you are loved

a beginner's
guide
to the universe

a beginner's
guide
to the universe

uncommon ideas
for living an
unusually happy life

mike dooley

HAY HOUSE, INC.
Carlsbad, California • New York City
London • Sydney • New Delhi

Published in the United States by: Hay House, Inc.: www.hayhouse.com®
Published in Australia by: Hay House Australia Pty. Ltd.: www.hayhouse.com.au
Published in the United Kingdom by: Hay House UK, Ltd.: www.hayhouse.co.uk
Published in India by: Hay House Publishers India: www.hayhouse.co.in

Cover design: Kathleen Lynch • *Interior design:* Bryn Starr Best
Images used under license from Shutterstock.com
Photograph on page 167: courtesy of the author

Library of Congress Cataloging-in-Publication Data

Names: Dooley, Mike, 1961- author.
Title: A beginner's guide to the universe : uncommon ideas for living an
    unusually happy life / Mike Dooley.
Description: 1st Edition. | Carlsbad : Hay House, Inc., 2019.
Identifiers: LCCN 2018049677 | ISBN 9781401955021 (hardcover : alk. paper)
Subjects: LCSH: Life--Miscellanea. | Wisdom--Miscellanea.
Classification: LCC BF1999 .D6152 2019 | DDC 158--dc23 LC record available at
https://lccn.loc.gov/2018049677

Hardcover ISBN: 978-1-4019-5502-1
e-book ISBN: 978-1-4019-5503-8
Audiobook ISBN: 978-1-4019-5591-5

10 9 8 7 6 5 4 3 2 1
1st edition, March 2019

Printed in the United States of America

To Rebecca Solecito Dooley

Before this odyssey ever began,

there was you, your best friends,

and wide-eyed curiosity among you about who would be

the first to leap,

the first to forget, the first to kiss, the first to tell,

the first to fall, the first to get back up,

and the first to remember

that living in the illusions of time and space

all began with a dare . . .

. . . to LOVE in spite of it all.

contents

the man
you
think i am

Dearest Rebecca,

The phone call I'll never forget came late afternoon at home. It was the weekend, I was sitting at the desk in my office, your mother across from me. A nurse began, "You want to know the sex?"

"What?"

"You and your wife are having a baby," she explained patiently, "and you want to know the sex?"

"Yes! Right!"

Without a hint of emotion, she continued, "You're going to have a girl."

It was as if God had just spoken.

This reality check of our firstborn about to arrive, when I was 52 years of age (soon to be 53), seemed more authentic than the modestly increased curvature of your mother's belly.

A GIRL!

My entire life, while outwardly nonchalant about having kids at all, I'd sometimes allow myself to imagine having a daughter. Of course, by my age, it seemed this boat had already sailed.

And then you arrived, six weeks early. Evading the 25 percent chance you had, based on your mom's and my genetics, of having full-blown cystic fibrosis. Your five and a half pounds turning our family of two into three. Your mother's existence, and mine, about to be transformed in ways unimaginable, never mind that we'd been warned of this by every parent who's ever lived. Even today, my greatest surprise over your presence in our lives is how surprised I've been *by everything*.

As I held you the first time, your searching eyes belied a depth not apparent in your extremely small, frail body. This window to your soul gave no hint of where you've been, the plans you've made, or who you might become. Your tiny limbs and quivering voice were angelic. I was mesmerized. Which had less to do with odds beaten and digits counted, and more with your very embodiment of life's greatest mystery: How could *any* of this—LIFE, YOU, our new family—be *remotely* possible?!

As these first years have rolled by and your fifth birthday now approaches, more than anything else, I'm awed as I witness you taking your place in the world: vessel of spirit, spark of the Divine. Not as "my" child—you are not truly "mine"—but as a child of the Universe. Still confounded that your mother and I somehow caused a biological chain of events, far beyond our ability to grasp, that would deliver you, as if from heaven, into our lives. That we are charged as caregivers and light bearers seems so contrarily absurd. Who are we to deserve so much? And who are we to be given so great a task? I fumble in my own darkness enough—there's not much light to spare. Yet, that this madness is so, parents in the dark bringing forth children of light, in a world of *meticulous order*, means there must be a plan and reason for our relationship. And so I will endeavor, as all parents must, to fulfill my role and not take more from you than I'm able to give.

Since your arrival I've adored you for every reason and for none at all. And, as if things could be even better, to my wild astonishment, you seem to be just as crazy about me. To the point of embarrassment as you shun others who crave your attention as much as I do, and when you reach for me in spite of their outstretched arms and open, vulnerable hearts.

Has there been some cosmic mistake that I, rather than a misplaced saint, am the one so privileged to enjoy the extreme proximity of your existence and these mutual currents of adoration, punctuated with giggles and tears? If only—my heart sometimes aches—I could be the man you think I am when you urgently and repeatedly call out, "Daddy! Daddy! Daddy!" *hundreds* of times in a single day, wanting to share with me your every observation, idea, or whim. Or when you cry over my absence, want to ride upon my shoulders, or sit beside me for a meal. How could *I* be so important to such perfection as you?

This importance is what I now strive to earn. To one day become the man you see in me—the man you think I am—and to always be a light in your darkness, hope in your despair, and the best father in the world to any degree I may.

When your mom was still pregnant I was told by a friend that your impending birth would mark the day my life would begin. And so it seems—so much so, that I sometimes feel my time on earth prior to your arrival was merely preparation for what we're now experiencing and all that lies ahead.

Speaking of which, while I have every expectation of loving and guiding you for decades more, I'm not so naïve to think you'll hear all I say, to assume what I offer will actually be helpful, or, to even be sure I'll live that long. Yet, as an author and speaker, whose "Notes from the Universe" have almost made me famous, and whose ideas have at least improved *my* own life, there are some things I hope to impart before this gig is up . . . or before we find out there really was some cosmic mistake. As if, *a beginner's guide to the universe*—a handbook for rocking these hallowed jungles of time and space as a budding master, with uncommon ideas for living an unusually happy life.

Not that I'm a master, but my work the past two decades has been to help people live deliberately and create consciously among life's infinite possibilities—à la *thoughts become things*, my catchphrase in the film and book *The Secret*. I've been teaching that life is neither a random game of chance, nor a test of obedience. That we live in a world of absolute perfection, made possible by love, upon which we are inclined to thrive. I actually tell audiences that life is *not* fair, but rigged in our favor.

To add some girding to these otherwise woo-woo ideas, my style and tone have always been more certified public accountant than doting father. I'm simply not used to exploring love and tenderness, which makes all that I feel for you so bizarre and tantalizing. But in spite of my actuarial tone (which I do think serves the lessons), I hope to reach both your mind *and* your heart.

I realize, of course, most people these days don't read books, and I've found this is triply true if the author is a family member. "Never a prophet in your hometown." In your own *home*? Forget it . . . *"and would you please take out the trash?"* That's fine—I'd rather be your dad than your guru. Still, teaching is what I've been doing and loving for 20 years. And, if the things I write could possibly shorten your own learning curves, lessen future suffering, and increase future joys, I must try.

In the pages that follow, there are six chapters covering the key tenets and concepts that I believe, once known, will give you or any reader the biggest boost possible in life.

Each chapter is introduced by a letter recalling my own life's epiphanies or relating memories of times recently shared together, followed by brief lessons on taking massive responsibility and its immense rewards. Finally, the epilogue will let you in on the most surprising discovery I've made from compiling these ideas, perhaps even the most surprising discovery of my life, concerning the shortcoming that weighs on me most lately—not being the man you think I am—a revelation with implications for every single person who's ever lived.

So, to spare you any guilt that might arise from blowing off my 15 earlier books, this single one, as simple and concise as I could make it, capturing what I'd most hope any avid reader would gain from all my books combined, is for you . . . and for anyone else who'd like to be reminded of life's beauty, our power, and how much we're loved.

**May all that you
wish for
be the least you
receive.**

1

why the
sun
rises

Tears and fears filled a large part of your early life.

You still cry for Mumu, though Mom passed when you were one year old. It was her knees you'd cling to when learning to walk. Her 81-year-old frame you'd yearn to hug. Her tired face you'd eagerly kiss.

Three years ago, you screamed, "Daddy! Help! A-a-a-a-a-a-a-a-a-a-a-a-g-h!" from the guest bathroom, where moments later I found you, having reached into the empty tub and tipped yourself in, like a seesaw, landing on your extended palms, head down, feet high, your miniature, inverted frame frozen in terror, unable to move except to call for help.

And you woke us on several nights last year, still half asleep, crying with punctuated persuasion, "I . . . DON'T . . . LIKE . . . MONSTERS!"

Crying, obviously, is a child's tribal call for answers, solutions, or love—that, in each case, must be provided by others. Needs that get more complicated as we age, because while we outgrow many of our dependencies, we still find more to be afraid of.

Fear's been my lifelong companion and nemesis. Mostly worrying about things that never happened, my own inadequacy, or what other people are thinking. Yet I've learned how to cope and even to thrive, loved and in love, by discovering that all fears stem from misunderstandings. And that just a few, new, on-point ideas, applied to painful circumstances or sad perspectives, can completely change everything for the better.

The most powerful lesson I may have ever learned came with the realization that at the core of *all fear* lies confusion over *who we really are, why we're here, and what we can do with our lives.* Which may seem unlikely, until you find out those answers. Ironically, when not tragically, the truths we miss that could steer us clear of confusion are easy to observe and experience in our own day-to-day lives.

Our physical senses alone reveal we live in an infinitely kind and unspeakably wise Universe that we are a part of, not apart from; where you, yourself, through mere thoughts, words, and deeds, become a creator. And of our countless creations, our lives are one.

Getting more cerebral, if Einstein was right and reality is merely a "persistent illusion," then by extension, so must be time, space, and matter. He said as much about these elements in lesser-known writings. Which means there are no real "befores," "afters," "nears," or "fars." Everything is literally "here and now," "One," with no spatial, material, or time separations. Such qualifiers merely offer unique windows of selective perception.

So, in a Universe without separations, where all are truly One, mustn't we each be made of, come from, Divine Intelligence? Without separations there can't be God and non-God. Where would non-God "stuff" come from, anyway? And being of God means you, or your higher self, existed "before" this lifetime and you will "after" it; it means you are real, the illusions are not; you are forever, they are fleeting. It means you came first. Yet that you now find yourself within time and space means you (your higher self) must have chosen to be here and now!

To continue using simple logic, we can conversely realize that amid life's staggering sophistication, it's not feasible that we're here to be tested, judged, and sentenced by an angry, jealous God. First, a God who could dream up the entire universe, much less photosynthesis, could not possibly be so petty, and second, what purpose would testing achieve? To see if God made a mistake?!

Similarly, it's easy to nix the old notion that life started because of some random accident and is devoid of intelligence. That's the same as believing that life sprang from rocks or vacuums,

without explaining the origin of rocks and vacuums, while casting a blind eye to the intelligence within the world's 100 million *different
species*, and every cell, in their every body.

All of which builds to the inescapable conclusion that
you are important; sacred, honored, loved, not beholden to
a world of illusions; rather, it is beholden to you. You are a
creator, through the act of perception, of every rock and
vacuum; they did not create you. *YOU are the very reason
the sun comes up every day.* Literally. Not "sort of" the reason, but *the* reason. You are free. Just be yourself. There
are no tests. All is well. *You deserve happiness, the indisput-
able highest emotional value known to humankind.* (Love is
not an emotion, but an absolute, as you'll read later.) And
while these ideas may raise major questions that neither of
us has answers for, given the insights just acquired, do those
questions matter anymore?

My evidence? How do I know the truth? As your father,
I consider it my highest duty to help you think for yourself
and to thrive in the world. And to that end, I'm simply
offering for your consideration some of the ideas that I've
honored and lived to great success. Ideas based on love and
respect for all. Hardly my own, yet so universal and self-
evident they can easily be attained by any earnest seeker.

My "process" for uncovering truth, which in hindsight
always passes a simple two-prong test:

Begin with an idea that electrifies you, sourced from
your own experiences, logic, or intuition, and consider it
true if it:

- speaks of life's beauty or our power, and

- applies to everyone, always, equally,
  no matter what.

No one is left behind, no one is excluded, no one is judged.

Could there be better confirmations for truth than our own experiences, logic, and intuition? It might be easy to brush these off as amateurish, until you consider that today's predominant beliefs do *not* pass their muster and have no rational basis other than to further scare and manipulate the masses.

If there were better qualifiers of truth, what would they be? Books? Priests? Scientists? Aren't texts, creeds, and theories merely summaries of other people's findings? Better for you to experience life, go within, *draw your own conclusions* and then see how they stand up to those drawn by a few of the world's most revered, unbiased thinkers like Lao-tzu, Confucius, Plato, Socrates, Aristotle, Seneca, Marcus Aurelius, Descartes, Emerson, Thoreau, James, Nietzsche, Hesse, Gibran, or the *thousands* of other respected voices from history for confirmation. I hope this book one day gives your own experiences, logic, and intuition such confirmation as well. Not that you need *any* authority other than yourself to stake your claim on life's unquestionable beauty and your immutable power.

I'm aware, of course, that putting words to truth can sometimes limit it. Due to this unavoidable language barrier, you're about to find subtle yet unavoidable *seeming* contradictions throughout this book. Yet, I'd rather risk minor and temporary confusion to buck you from herd-like thinking, and to spark your own search for answers.

As you weigh and consider all I've written, call out the limitations and contradictions, but also find what resonates with your heart, aligns with your mind, and is evident in your life. When you discover an idea for which there's no such resonance, assuming enough of this book does, let it be an invitation for your own sense of personal responsibility to ask, "If this isn't the truth, *then what is*?"

If I convince you of nothing else, I will have succeeded if you grasp the immensity of your duty to ask that follow-up question for all things in life that trouble your heart, knowing that there is *always* a single answer to find and leverage for your own peace and happiness.

There are no other rules. There are no hidden agendas. And there are no unknown variables working against you. You truly do have dominion over all things, unmitigated by *anything* . . . except confusion over what the truth is.

Your "rock" this lifetime will come from understanding the most fundamental absolutes of our reality, which is what this chapter is about. Then, fear can be banished from your life and all good things added—peace, comfort, creativity, confidence, health, wealth, friendships, happiness, love, enlightenment, truly *all things*.

Which is exactly what I wish for you.

You're not here to earn your
wings,
you're here because, in some long-forgotten realm,
you already did.

You came first.
Before the sun, the moon, and the stars
You chose to be here.
You're who you most wanted to be.

The reason you forget who you were
before
this lifetime began,
is to more fully be who you now are.

"Reality" is not that you're weak,
and dream of becoming strong;
poor, and dream of becoming rich;
alone, and dream of having friends.
It's that you're strong, rich, and among friends—
yet, at times, dream that you're not.

Thinking is life's only **variable**.
Everything else was settled a long,
long time ago.

In the most **basic** sense,
life as we know it **began**
when God set out, through us,
to think what has never been **thought.**

You are God's *only* chance to be **you**.
To **see** what no one else will ever see,
to **hear** what no one else will ever hear,
and to **think** and feel what no one else will
ever think and **feel.**
You are more precious than you can possibly **imagine.**

You're already one of the most
important
people who will ever live.

The "original sin" was seeing the world of illusions
and thinking they formed reality;
Adam biting into the proverbial, illusionary, apple
as if it was real,
and thus falling from grace,
falling from truth.

Every time we react to the world around us
as though *it* were reality,
we eat of the forbidden fruit.

If you look to time and space
for answers, direction, and meaning,
they'll rock your world in every which way.
Yet discover they look to *you* for answers,
direction, and meaning,
and you will rock the world.

The more you believe in appearances,
in the story told by your physical senses,
and see yourself as a pawn in the circumstances
you now find yourself in,
the less control you'll have over them.
By all means enjoy appearances,
just don't trust them.

It's not the "unseen" that's fiction,
        but the **seen**.
What you can touch will one day disappear;
        what you can feel will last **forever**.

The **truth** will not only set you free,
        it'll slay all dragons, banish all fears,
            heal what hurts, fill what's empty,
        clear what's confused, connect all dots,
lighten what's heavy, bring friends together,
        turn **dust** to gold,
            and raise the **sun**.

To **see** more and more of what we're missing
        fully explains the **evolution** of consciousness
        within time and space.

All deliberate change comes first from
denying the logic that earlier
gave you comfort.

Our ability to stop kidding ourselves
is what brings about the greatest
breakthroughs, fastest comebacks,
and happiest feet.

True love is a given, not an option;
an absolute, not a variable.
Born of our divinity, not our humanity.
Always unconditional.

Our lives are not about love,
they're about our adventures into love.
Our adventures are the variable,
not love.

Life is not just what you see, but what you've projected.
It's not just what you feel,
but what you've decided.
It's not just what you've experienced,
but how you've remembered it.
It's not just what you've forged, but what you've allowed.
And it's not just who's appeared,
but who you've summoned.

One of the greatest paradoxes of your physical senses is
that they actually show you what you believe,
as much as what you perceive—
fortunately, the former is easier to change.

Instead of running from something scary,
it's easier to learn not to be scared of it.

It's impossible to be scared when you dwell in truth.

Usually, loving more is easier than
fearing less and gets better results.

You can only be afraid,
> when you pretend you're not in control.
Lonely, when you stop doing **things.**
> Bored, when you stop following your heart.
And overwhelmed, when you think
> the **illusions** are real.

The believed-in **myth** that you might somehow lose
> or become less is what makes **life** an adventure.

Fear goes away when you remember:
> First, you're a **spiritual** being. And,
second, nothing can ever be
> lost or taken from a spiritual being
> > that cannot be **re-created.**

Sometimes it takes being pressed with darkness
> **before** you begin to seek the light.

Life does not **happen** to you.
> **You** happen to life.

While you'll often hear that change is life's only constant,
the only thing really changing
is you and what you understand.

Time and space are simply measures of self-awareness.

For those whose thoughts are free,
so is everything else.
Whether or not they know it.

Whatever you want,
you deserve.

All forms of separation—
disconnects, divides, illnesses, partings,
breakups, and good-byes
—are temporary.

You are forever.

If speaking to a spiritual novice
    during the **earliest** days of human evolution,
you might explain God, metaphorically,
    as if "He" were angry, testing, and judgmental.

To someone a bit more savvy,
    during **easier** times, you might explain God,
metaphorically, as if "She" were always loving, nurturing,
    and forever conspiring on your behalf.

And to someone on the verge of total enlightenment,
    during the **latter** days of human evolution,
you might explain God by asking them
    to turn up the **music,**
take off their **shoes,**
    walk in the **grass,**
unleash the dog,
    free the canary,
catch a breeze,
    ride upon a wave,
dream upon a star,
    dance
    every day,
get up early, take a nap, stay out late,
    eat chocolate,
feel the **love,**
    give stuff **away,**
earn it back,
    give some more,
and **laugh.**

Heaven is everywhere, **always**, at once.
Hell is **not** knowing it.

Find the good in *every* circumstance. It's always there.

Behold God, **everywhere,** always, now.
There's no devil, nor does evil exist
of its own device.
Evil is simply ignorance in human **thought,**
misdiagnosed.

While there will be no such thing as a "Judgment Day,"
there are **consequences.**
And the consequences of misunderstanding life's truths
are **likely** to include poor behavior,
repeating cycles, and, possibly, a truly harrowing
adventure through time and space . . .
until your thinking aligns with **truth.**
Which will only ever lie
a few new **thoughts** away.

No matter how long you ignore life's magic
or unwittingly swim against its current,
the instant you stop struggling
you'll be back in the flow,
the prodigal child returned home,
inheritance fully restored.

There are only three things you need
to know about angels:

1. They're real.
2. Some exist to serve you.
3. They can do the most when you ask them for help.

Just because you're a
supernatural,
unstoppable, creator doesn't mean you can't have
friends on your team who help you out
from time to time.

Avoid gray areas.
   Therein, the **pathway** to safety and comfort
is guarded by the unreliable half-truths of
      "maybe," "sometimes," and "I don't know."

Life is absolute and its principles are **exacting.**
      In all things, there is *a* truth.

See everything through **truth's** light
      and you'll never know sadness, lack, or limits.
You'll see that you are safe. Bathed in **love.**
      Surrounded by admirers in both
            the physical and spiritual realms.
You'll see only beauty, perfection, and **meaning.**
      And you'll realize that just as the stark contrasts
of time and space may seem to imprison you, within them
      lies their own **infinite** possibilities.

Nothing will free you more than the **truth**
      and nothing will hold you back more
            than not **knowing** it.

If you **ever** get curious and wonder
who you were meant to be,
look in the mirror and **smile.**

Your life's **purpose** is far more
a function of being yourself,
than making clever **choices.**

Feeling lost does not **mean** you are.

All that you **need,** to have all that you want,
lies inside of you right **now.**

While the notions of purpose, meanings, and destinies
may **challenge** you,
one idea you can always be clear on is that the mind
that spun the **cosmos** together
clearly has wishes and dreams all its own
. . . that obviously included you.

All is **supremely** well.

There is no choice you will ever make that might
limit you as much as you may fear.

Busy yourself doing what you most want,
among the possibly skimpy choices
you'll **sometimes** have,
and in no time you'll find that
your purpose has found you.

What's most important is that you're here.
A million times less important is
what you do here, when, **where,** and with whom.

You are not on earth to make things happen . . .
to spread the love . . . to make it a better place
or to learn acceptance of the things you cannot change.
You are not on earth to find your soulmate
or your **purpose**
. . . To put the needs of others before your own.
And you are most certainly not on earth to suffer,
pay penance, be tested, or **judged** . . .

. . . you are here because in your loftiest state of being,
perched high above the wonderment,
at the pinnacle of your glory,
you wondered what it would be like,
even fleetingly, to believe in limits.

And when you can grasp this
from within the illusions,
you will also grasp how unlimited you truly are.

There are really only two conditions
of the human experience:
Very, very happy, or, about to become very, very happy.

"Your happiness" is the ultimate answer to every
"WHY?" you could ever ask God.

Forever has only just begun.
Slow never fails to arrive.
And, happy always lasts longer than sad.
Time truly is on your side.

Happiness doesn't mean you've settled for less;
   it means you're **ready** for more.

Some **people** are happiest when they're unhappy.
   Let them be **happy.**

If you ever want to find a life partner,
   live in **greater** prosperity, be more productive,
foster peace on earth, or improve your health,
   if you can "be happy now," ahead of time,
before these things have **arrived,**
   then these things will arrive even faster.

Happiness isn't a crop you harvest when
   your dreams come **true.**
It's the fertilizer that makes them come true faster.
   It's also what opens the floodgates, beats your heart,
finds true love, feeds your mind, and **frees** your soul.

The **wiser** you are, the easier life gets.
    But then, the happier you are,
the less you need easy.

By all means, seek to change the things you don't like
    and to manifest the things you do,
just don't put off your happiness for either.

Happiness is the **one** option you'll always have
    that no one can deny **you**.

The Law of Happy states:
    However happy you've ever been,
        you will one **day** be happier.

The **path** to enlightenment is not a path at all,
    but a metaphor for the **time** it takes to live in joy,
no matter **what.**

When the world seems hard and clarity is elusive,
    you might refresh your thinking by reframing
time and space as the kindergarten of the Universe,
    not its Harvard.

Rising suns and babbling brooks.
    Tropical forests and sleeping meadows.
Modern marvels and scientific breakthroughs.
    Exciting discoveries and limitless frontiers.
Devoted friends and caring strangers.
    Lives and loves and souls to hold so close,
your heart could burst . . .

While there may, at times, seem to be a lot of
    "real estate" between where you are
and where you dream of being,
    the road runs straight through paradise.

It's not that you have to wait
    for your dreams to come true,
but that you get to—
    in a magical world where love abounds,
in the palm of God's hand,
    until your brief turn in space is over.

The **reason** butterflies float, fireflies light,
    comets fall, trees grow, cats purr, and tails wag
is because each is **reflecting** something in you,
    at the very moment of perception,
disguised by the elements, captured in time,
    to remind you of your sublime **divinity.**

If you ever find yourself driving down the motorway of life,
    looking for an exit that says "Easy Street" . . .
consider, that's **probably** where we got on,
    following a sign that said, "Paradise, this way
Road Under Construction. **Watch** out for lightworkers,
    invisible beliefs, and runaway dogma. No stopping."

The **great** perfection of living a lifetime
    within a world of **illusions** lies in the fact that
no matter what happens next, you'll be richer for it.

People, when given a chance, smile, skip, and dance.
    They create, play, and laugh.
They care, share, and love.

The ones who don't, haven't yet realized that chances
    are something you give to yourself.

No matter your path,
    you will one day see that the good and the beautiful
wildly exceeded the bad and the ugly.

Should you ever overhear someone say
    they're only human,
remind them it's just for a short while, that before long
    they'll be able to see their wings again,
speak in tongues, and blaze trails throughout eternity
    upon chariots of fire.

The dead do have their day,
    and they all live beyond it.
No one really dies.

To the **naked** eye death appears random.
　　To the spiritually inclined it appears **ordained.**

Life is so magnificent that once you pass from this plane,
　　even your times of sorrow, fear, frustration, anger,
confusion, and loneliness will be dearly missed.

But you'll **smile** when you find them as carefully set jewels
　　in your crown of **compassion.**

You'll cry happy tears as the veils of time fall away
　　　revealing that each moment of the life you just lived
is still **unfolding**.

And you'll laugh when you **realize** this all could have
　　been understood when you were who you now are.

The odd thing about the often long and lonely path of life
　　is that when you get to the end of it and look back,
　　you'll find that it was neither.

Do not fear that at the end of your life,
   you will somehow disappear back into God
the way a cube of sugar dissolves into a hot drink,
   for even now you live your life inside of God,
while at the same time maintaining your own
   radiant essence and glorious identity.

Given the world's uncertainty
   about what happens at death,
it's easy to imagine that the main thing those who've
   "passed"would like to tell those who haven't is
that once you get over the shock of your safe arrival—
   completely intact, cool as ever, bathed in love—
what you'll miss most about Earth
   is the beguiling romance of uncertainty.

Not that you won't also miss windy mornings, starry skies,
   and old trees; bare feet, barking dogs, and beige;
beetles, strawberries, and doorbells; coffee, blue jeans,
   and falling leaves.

It's good to remember that all roads lead "home."
   It's better to realize that you never really left.

2

how
"things"
happen:

the logistics of magic & miracles

I remember hearing your heart beat for the first time, months before you were born. A heartbeat where earlier there'd been none. It was like hearing spirit knock on a door that would eventually open to time and space. "Miracle" fails to adequately describe the transformation of spirit into flesh.

And ever since, your presence and growth has ushered before us a procession of magical moments. Truly, if human beings only knew of how many miracles they performed every day, just by being here, nothing else in our lives would ever again overwhelm us, frighten us, or seem impossible.

Another one of my life's big "Aha!" moments, was finding that miracles need not bend the physical laws of the universe to blow our minds or leave us speechless. Most don't. And as you learn to create consciously, you'll actually begin to notice, with hindsight, that most of your extraordinary accomplishments will occur through an implausible, though wholly ordinary, series of events.

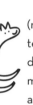

For example, dreaming of Prince Charming (no hurry, please), when followed with consistent, thoughtful action, unclouded with misunderstandings and contradictions, *will* lead to meeting Prince Charming . . . although through a seemingly natural sequence of "routine" events, that "coincidentally" lined up, each absolutely crucial and exquisitely timed, *that never would have occurred without the initial dream*. This is because all manifestations begin with a desired *end result*, which then *attracts* the right ideas, circumstances, and people onto your path. Ultimately creating a life that resembles, *or surpasses*, whatever you were originally thinking about.

Most miracles remain invisible and are unknown until long after they transpire. Yet you perform them all the time, we all do. Human beings are nonstop, can't-be-turned-off-even-if-we-wanted-to-be, natural-born creators. We are *matter manipulators* by way of our everyday thoughts, because these are the de facto *end results* that we end up believing in and acting on.

Of course, at first it doesn't seem possible that we could be "happening" to life in this way. Too many things we wish for never show up and too many things we never imagined do. You're sure to have as many objections and questions as I once did. But as you stay with it, insisting upon truth, opening heart and mind, you'll finally see the obvious:

- Thoughts become things, unless other thoughts of yours get in the way.

- When the unthought-of happens, it's always a stepping-stone in a journey to a farther destination *that you had thought of.*

- Shared manifestations, in a world of 7+ billion co-creators, like the weather or the economy, arise based on the participants' collective thoughts, confusions, and behaviors.

- Before this lifetime began, you knew the prevailing collective thoughts, and therefore the world's probabilities for war or peace, feast or famine, and other transformations or upheavals, as well as localized probabilities like how your parents might be challenged and how your other family members might live their lives. These either played into your life's private intentions or were irrelevant.

- It's usually "impossible" for a personal manifestation to violate core collective beliefs about the nature of reality, like the physical laws of the world. Were this to happen, it would tear the fabric of your collective life stage. Because of this, you can't turn charging lions into house cats. But your thoughts followed by action, like possessing an intense focus on survival and running for your life, might trigger a herd of passing zebras to distract those lions—which would be no less miraculous.

- While the collective may deny you certain freakish manifestations (like turning lions into kitties) and while you may temporarily give your power away to certain individuals, no one can ultimately keep you from manifesting more friends and laughter, health and healing, wealth and abundance, or living a happy, fulfilling life.

And it gets better.

A lot better.

Almost unimaginably better.

Your positive thoughts are far more likely to become "things" than your negative ones.

If this sounds over the top, consider: Haven't you smiled more than you've frowned? Laughed more than you've cried? Had clarity more than confusion? Friends more than enemies? Health more than sickness? Money more than being in the red? And in all such comparison, aren't the differences usually by GIGANTIC proportions? Can you then begin to see that life is not some 50/50 roll of the dice? That it's "not fair"? That nothing from your past can prevent you from thinking and thus creating anew?

Positive thoughts are in alignment with the beauty and power that brought us here. Thinking "positive" is going with the flow, instead of resisting it. That's why it has more power. Even part-time positivity will overrule part-time negativity, so long as there's both in thought and deed.

You are not expected to become a miracle worker. You already are one. Should spirit move you to explore this further, however, I urge you to begin noticing exactly how you've been "accidentally" doing what you do, and to start doing it deliberately, consciously, and with abandon. The lessons in this chapter will get you grounded in understanding the logistics of creation, opportunity, moving beyond limits, and your power over life's illusions. We'll take these concepts further in chapter 4 with lessons on how to apply them.

Fortify what you learn here with the evidence that's now everywhere in your life. We're literally built to thrive. *You're built to thrive.* It's our default setting *in absolutely all regards.* As wildly successful as the human race has been so far, *it's been so in spite of our profound naivetes—thinking that God is angry or that we're here by accident!* Can you imagine the scale of breakthroughs we'll experience once everyone sees the obvious, releases fear, and engages their power? This is where we're headed, and that day swiftly approaches.

I want it for you now.

No **matter** what you may go after in life,
getting what you want will always boil down to at least
a little bit of Divine Intervention—*your own.*

The **speed** with which any dream may be realized
is always a function of how small the miracles have to be
in order not to freak out the **dreamer.**

The **difference** between "have" and "have-not"
is always down to imagination.

There are **three** things that will
always evade your physical senses:
trees growing, the earth spinning,
and dreams coming **true.**
Never assume these things aren't happening
based upon what you see.

Detours, challenges, and crises are simply cover for
miracles that had no other way of reaching you.

Don't let the miracles that have not transpired yet,
blind you to those that have.

Your dreams are what the Universe
has dreamed for you.

Most miracles aren't obvious
until long after they happen,
which likely means that in your life, as you read these
words, some big ones have recently happened
that will soon change everything.

At all times, far more is happening on your behalf
than your physical senses will ever reveal.

While **knowledge** is indeed power,
    very little must be known
to dream, act, manifest, and be **happy.**

Wanting more is just the first sign
    of many that you're going to get it.

"**Thoughts** become things"
    explains where you fit into
the equation of reality **creation.** As a *creator* yourself.

What **mortals** don't realize is that for every
    thought they think the **physical** world is changed.
Not knowing this is the main thing that makes us mortal.

Nothing will change your life as much as
    changing your **mind.**

Until you dream, there isn't a mold.

Until you speak, there isn't a promise.

And until you move, there isn't a path.

Yet do these things, and you'll rearrange
the stars that shine on your life.

Divine Intelligence did not create the physical universe
by studying quarks, drawing schematics,
or painting butterflies.

It began by imagining the desired end result:
the vastness, the harmony, the symbiotic relationships,
a stage to play out our lessons,
and in an instant, Big Bang.

Everything necessary for life as we know it,
including the supporting math, sciences, and physical
laws of the universe, was spontaneously created
and forced into place.

Your chosen "end results" will do the same,
forcing the details, circumstances, people,
serendipities, accidents, and coincidences that will
ultimately bring about the manifestation of
your earlier thoughts.

Your net worth will depend mostly
    on your net thoughts.

The concepts of destiny, fate, luck, coincidences,
    and accidents are all contrary or subordinate to
the inviolate principle of *thoughts becoming things,*
    and will therefore always fail to fully explain
the life that you lead.

Ancient spiritual contracts
    of the kind you will no doubt read of,
do indeed exist and provide a framework
    for every facet of the life you'll lead.
However, they're rewritten every dawn,
    perpetually updated as each day unfolds,
and all stipulate they're to become null and void
    in the event they might ever limit you.

Karma is a phenomenon, not a law,

that contributes to the manifestation of your life
and circumstances *reflective of your focus, behavior, and beliefs.*

If your focus, behavior, and beliefs are
negative or positive, generous or stingy,

you will give and receive accordingly;
what goes around will indeed come around.

But change your focus, behavior, and beliefs and
you'll immediately begin to change your experiences,

regardless of any karmic "score."

Nothing that's happened in your past can take from

your present power to choose new thoughts,
create a new life, and be happy.

Our beliefs are almighty

because they inspire or shut down our thinking,
and it's the thoughts our beliefs encourage or shut down

that can or can't then become the things
and events of our lives.

While your beliefs will mostly be invisible,
    what they manifest will appear everywhere
        in your life.
You simply need to look at those areas that displease you
    to find where you might begin with some
introspection, probing, and rethinking.

One way to defeat invisible, limiting beliefs
    is to dream *and move* toward a life so grand
that the only way those new thoughts could become things
    is if any beliefs in their way were obliterated.
        And so they shall be.

Your beliefs are only invisible when you
    live within their limits.
Better to reach, stretch, and dream big.

Just because you might not know what your
    limiting beliefs are,
you can always know the kinds of empowering beliefs
    you'd like to possess.
Write these down. Get used to them. See their validity.
    And then, one decision at a time, one day at a time,
choose to behave with the mind of the highest within
    you. Until that's all there is.

Your **words** are your thoughts
        that will become things the soonest—
    let them be of what you like and love.
What you care about and **cherish.**
        What serves you and makes you happy.
What gives you wings and makes your heart sing.
        What makes you **dream.**
And very little else.

A **focus** on undesirable circumstances
        will usually extend and **multiply** those circumstances.

When you **talk** about "what is" or "what was,"
        even if just explaining to a friendly ear,
you risk projecting **more** of the same into your future.

When you truly understand how **life** works,
you'll rarely, if ever, say things like, "It's hard,"
        "It's not working," or "Something's wrong with me."

Instead, you'll start saying things like,
        "I'll find the time for that." "Good thing I'm rich."
or "I can't take a bad picture."

The **emotional** highs and lows
of any given day reveal **exactly**
what you've been telling yourself on that **day.**

The **mason,** disappointed with the form of fresh
concrete, does not try to **reshape** it;
she starts over.

Often, having what you want
is a function of mentally letting **go** of what you have.

Just because you're not being judged,
doesn't mean you live in a world that's
neutral to your existence.
You are loved, supported, and inclined to succeed.

Your **positive** thoughts are at least 10,000 times more
powerful than your negative thoughts.

Don't **worry** that you worry.
Even the fewest positive thoughts,
words, and steps taken, **every** day,
can turn any tide and right any ship.

Self-correcting, rebounding, and healing
are both in your nature and **entirely** normal.

The **best** hope one has for thriving among the seen,
the known, and the manifested
comes from playing off the **unseen,** the unknown,
and the not yet manifested.

There's always more than one right answer,
path, possibility, partner, nuance, or flavor—
so insist upon none, or you'll **exclude** all others.

It's not the day you have to manage, but the **moment.**
It's not the dragon you have to slay, but the fear.
And it's not the path you have to **know,**
but the destination.

The "Bermuda Triangle of Manifesting"
      contains 3 "things" you can never be assured
of successfully micromanaging:
      specific people behaving in *specific* ways,
            how a dream will come true,
                  and unimportant details
(by the way, all details are unimportant).

The workaround is simple:
      imagine **abundance,** not a dollar amount,
            love without insisting upon **who,**
                  and a **rocking** *life,*
not just bells, whistles, and bling.

To **safeguard** that you're not in
      the Bermuda Triangle of Manifesting,
punctuate the end of each expressed desire with
      "or better."

To insist upon whos, hows, wheres, and minutiae
      is to **limit** an otherwise unlimited Universe.
Dwell upon the WOWs, not the hows.

The problem with compromising,
　　　　economizing, and **settling** for less,
is that these results are no easier to manifest
　　　　than their fuller counterparts.

Life's **magic** has to work just as hard
　　　　whether the bar's been lowered or raised.

Don't be afraid to go where you've never gone
　　　　and do what **you've** never done,
because both are **necessary** to have what you've never had
　　　　and to be who you've never been.

It's not the **dazzling** voice that makes a singer.
　　　　Or clever stories that make a writer.
And it's not piles of money that make a tycoon.
　　　　It's having a dream and wanting to live it so **greatly**
that you'd rather move with it and "fail"
　　　　than succeed in another realm.

When the fear of **things** staying the same
exceeds the fear of failure,
things **happen**.

A **dream** not followed by consistent action,
points either to **thoughts** of contradiction
or misunderstandings.

Hoping, **wishing,** and praying
shouldn't ever be confused
with **doing.**

You were not **born** to wait.
You were born to **create.**

It **only** takes one second in time
for everything to **fantastically** change for the better,
and you're far more likely to have one such second
by *actively living* as many as you can.

Being **excited** about the truth
    is never enough to change your life.
You must physically live the **truth**.

You don't have to do "it" **right**,
    you just have to **do** "it."

The **next** step on your path to living the life
    of your wildest dreams will rarely lie behind doors
marked "WOW," "SEXY," or "GLAMOROUS."

Life's **magic** works through you.
    Not beside you. Not around you.
Not for you. Not instead of you.
      Through **you**.

In life, it's as if we each must choose
    from countless **doorways,**
        all leading to new and different pathways.
So we **wonder** and think, calculate and stress,
    over whether or not we'll knock on the "right" one.
But what we can't yet see is that all of the **pathways**
    beyond all of the doorways
        eventually lead to the same great room,
in the same great house, at the same great party.

Although there are exceptions,
    the **more** you do,
        the more will be **done** for you.

Taking massive action, on **massive** dreams,
    amid massive uncertainties, is pretty much where
anyone who's ever done anything massive had to **start.**
    And then things got way easier.

At any **point** in your life,
    the greater the uncertainties you face,
the greater your **chances** of hitting a major,
    life-changing "home run."

Changing what you have
    comes from changing who you are,
which comes from changing what you think,
    which comes from changing what you believe,
which are led by desire and action.

Simply wanting something reinforces the belief
    that you don't have what you want,
perpetuating that lack.
    Instead, name what you don't yet have by giving
thanks in advance for having received it,
    as if you already had.

When you give thanks for what you already have,
    the corresponding manifestation
        is to expand and increase what you have.
When you give thanks for what you don't have,
    as if you already had it,
        the corresponding manifestation is to attract
            and create it into your life.

Prayers that lack conviction, confidence,
    and end in question marks like,
        "Can I? May I? Will I?"
    get answers like, "Sure! You bet! No question!"

They don't get results.

    Which is fine, unless you wanted results.

Don't ask. Give thanks.

Giving heartfelt thanks for the good fortunes
    that befall others—no matter who they are
—will help yield similar good fortunes for you.

It's not wanting that unlocks wheels, parts seas,
                and changes everything.
It's expecting so greatly
    that you begin preparing
                and thanking in advance.

What you give, will be given to you.

To **find** out how much you've truly been blessed with
in terms of love, time, **energy,** or any other quality,
substance, or dispensation, give of them.
Then you'll know what **boundless** really means.

Giving demonstrates a belief you are provided for.
It's an act of **faith** that implies you will remain whole,
that what you gave will come back to you,
and that **love** is what matters most.

And when you believe these things they'll become your reality,
and abundance will be **showered** upon you
as if the **heavens** had opened up.

It's always **better** to give too much, pay too much,
and love too much than not enough,
especially when you understand it all comes **back** anyway.

Once **enlightened,** you can do less and have more.
But . . . once enlightened, who would want to do less
when you finally **realize** the world spins in your very hand,
our thoughts become things, and you can have, do,
or be anything you want when you **continually**
show up, stay active, and keep busy?

Unofficially, I'd say that the number-one cause of
loneliness is not a lack of friends,
but a lack of keeping busy.
And that nine out of ten times the solution to every
crisis, challenge, or problem—in relationships,
careers, or otherwise—is to get busy.

One out of ten times the solution will be to
first get quiet, and then get busy.

Little is more impressive, inspirational, or sexy than
watching someone in the throes of action,
driven by purpose, oblivious to all but their aim.
    And anyone, including you, can be that person,
on any day you choose.

It's easier to fall in love,
    and to be fallen in love with,
when you're busy.

The busier you are the faster time flies, the less you **worry**,
the more **friends** you have, the farther you travel,
the richer you become, the quicker you rebound,
and the happier you **feel.**
Plus, chances of being in the right place at the **right** time
increase exponentially. Not just for the improved odds,
but the improved **faith** it demonstrates.

You can only ever do what you can, with what you have,
from where you are. Yet by design,
it'll always be **enough.**

Usually, the best way to find the yellow brick road
of your **life** is to start out on the dusty dirt one.
And to let yourself become so preoccupied in making the **best**
of it, having **fun,** and challenging yourself
that you actually stop paying **attention** to the path.

Until, **one** day, not too long after you began,
with a new best friend, feeling awesome
and a teeny tiny bit taller, looking down at your **path**
you'll **notice** that it's "24 karats."

Then you'll **wonder** for a long time,
probably as you sip on an exotic fruit drink,
on what day the transformation **actually** took place.

You **may** not be able to take "it" with you
      at the end of your **life,**
but whatsoever you may do, be, or have in **time** and space
      awaits you on the ot**her** side.

The **path** to enlightenment
      usually includes many stages.
            Most commonly, it begins with
festering misunderstandings that lead to pain,
      the pain then leads to growth,
          growth leads to **clarity,**
              clarity leads to fun,
                  fun leads to joy,
             and joy leads to true **illumination.**

Whenever possible, and it usually is,
      I recommend skipping to the **fun** part.

3

learning from

all

that hurts

I bet it's a beautiful day when you read this. Not necessarily sunshiny and breezy, or even daylight, but sparkling with possibilities and laden with potential. They all are.

Just three years ago, part of my morning ritual, after changing and feeding you breakfast, was to take a short walk, carrying you past a few houses and back. In the winter I'd swaddle you in a blanket, and on warmer days leave your bare arms and legs to the morning's breeze.

You'd never fail to hold your head high, eyes wide, silently periscoping as I chronicled all I saw . . . from the rising sun, to overhead birds plying the sky, waving neighbors headed off to work, a snail crossing the sidewalk in front of us, peppered with flowery descriptions, observing and declaring that it was, yet another, *"Beautiful day!"*

By the time you were walking and talking, age three, some mornings, at the first sign of sunrise, you'd creep into our room and timidly ask with a sleep-strained voice, "Daddy . . . is . . . it . . . a bea-u-ti-ful day? Is it a bea-u-ti-ful day, Daddy?" And then as you heard us stir, gaining in tempo and excitement, you'd continue, *"Is it a beautiful day?! Is it a beautiful day?! Is it a beautiful day?!"* Not really questioning the day's beauty, but wanting to know if it was, in fact, a *new* day—confident, I choose to believe, in your early wisdom, that all days are beautiful.

Of course, *everything* that happens within every moment of any day is born of meaning, order, and love—the epitome of beauty. Even though sometimes, to the physical senses, things might appear to be anything but. That such seeming contradictions unexpectedly crop up, however, will not mean that you aren't solely creating your life nor will it mean that God is serving up "tests." We are our own teachers and there are no tests, as you'll soon read.

This is the trickiest chapter, because what's to be shared can seem naïve, negative, or just plain offensive. But consider, if you're beginning to understand that you live a life of your own creation, couched in love, then just maybe, the more any of these carefully vetted chapter lessons sting or offend, the more you have to learn. Life's perfection isn't part-time. It's all the time. And when we suffer it's always because *we've* missed something, not because we've found a flaw in the world. Yes, there's ugliness, but it's never pointless. Find the point and you'll close in on the healing; see the healing and you'll find love.

Accepting Responsibility

Coming to terms with your supernatural power, means accepting your supernatural responsibilities. To live full throttle, you must accept responsibility for *everything* that has ever happened to you. Including your birth and those experiences that were seemingly thrust upon you. If Prince Charming is not who you thought he'd be, move on, but also try to understand your beliefs about men and relationships that led you to define, want and choose him as you once did.

At first, this may seem unfair, to say the least. Yet life is an adventure into possibilities and experimentation. Everyone choosing to be alive at this early stage of our civilization's development made this choice knowing that ugly things might happen. Made possible, in part, by our own misunderstandings, at a time when unintentional manifestations would be the norm. But we also knew that we'd be surrounded by beauty and possibilities, in a world sustained by love. That we'd be able to change most circumstances we found displeasing. We also knew we'd "return home" unscathed, even greater for the experience, eternity still calling, no matter what had just happened in the fleeting, imaginary illusions of time and space.

By claiming responsibility for all things in your life, you reclaim your power. You no longer believe *that others, fate, or God decides what happens to you.* You cease being a victim. You begin living on your terms.

Life Lessons

All dreams come with built-in challenges. If not, you'd already have what you want and there'd be no dream. One does not exist without the other, but our challenges only reveal themselves once we start moving toward our dreams. For example, wanting your dream job, but finding it requires public speaking. Moving in with Romeo, to discover *he* wasn't quite ready. Wanting to write a book, then learning what that demands. Your dreams are part of how you will one day become the person you know you can be; they call you down a path upon which you learn "the price" you must pay for their realization. If you like, you can think of them as tests you must pass, but not given by God—created instead from the collision and juxtaposition of your old thoughts (that led to today) and your new ones (that will make your dreams come true).

With more critical thinking you'll see your challenges show you where your thoughts and beliefs need clarity. They are hurdles that perfectly match your evolution at the exact moment you're ready to take the next step. *This is how it works.* Your dreams aren't random, they're custom fitted (by you) to take you on a journey that will teach what *you* wanted to learn—maybe not consciously, but effectively. That's the whole point: your dreams lie beyond your reach, *so that you will reach!*

How I *desperately* wish that you'd never suffer the pain of a broken heart—never know what it is to be slighted, feel lost, unworthy, insufficient—the list of such agonies is endless. Yet when I reflect on my own life, I'm truly frightened by the thought of how much less I'd be today had such grievances been shielded from me, denying me the spiritual insights and emotional wisdom that have come from my own times of defeat, heartbreak, and humiliation. These scars have given my subsequent life quests traction and made possible achieving heights of love and confidence that earlier I couldn't even have imagined.

The emotional pains you'll inevitably encounter will hurt me every bit as much as they'll hurt you, but avoiding them is not the answer. Learning to rebound, grow, and flourish despite them is—which I hope to help you with through the following lessons. This chapter is about reframing how you view setbacks and problems, helping you to leverage the gifts that come from adversity, because no trifling of the past, no matter how great, can tarnish the brilliance of eternity.

Love you, mean it.

Always,
  the thing that didn't work out for your very, very best
. . . really did.

You didn't choose this lifetime
  thinking it would be without challenges.
You chose it, in large part,
  for the challenges you'd likely have.

When something troubling, difficult,
  or painful happens,
look to see what it makes possible,
  that wouldn't have otherwise been possible,
and you'll find at least part of its reason for happening.

The path to enlightenment must include:
  Accepting full responsibility for your own happiness.
  And,
accepting full responsibility
    for your own unhappiness.

It's one kind of **victory** to slay a beast,
  move a mountain, and cross a chasm;
it's another kind **altogether** to realize that the beast,
  the mountain, and the chasm
were of your own design.

If not for your **challenges,** problems, and issues,
  how else would you know there are still
a few things you **misunderstand**?

Every "no" **means** "not yet."
  Every setback means "there's something **better**."
Every loss means "even more is on the way."
  And every disappointment, "pucker up, buttercup."

It's not just that when one **door** closes,
  another door opens.
When one door closes, choirs burst into chorus,
  orchestras orchestrate, bugles bugle, pigs fly,
and 10,000 new doors **open**.

It's no one's **responsibility** to tell you
what your "issues" are,
and contrary to popular thinking, most will not.
Which pretty much means there'll only be
one person you can trust in such matters.

Where you are is never **who** you are.

You're not **alive** to face hurdle after hurdle;
it's not as if, should you master your issues today,
more will be added tomorrow.
While there'll always be more to learn, as you become
wiser you'll find you have fewer challenges,
which are each quite manageable,
feeling more like **opportunities** than burdens.

The only **real** problem you'll ever have
is thinking you have a problem.

When you prepare for adversity,
　　you build not a bridge to retreat by,
but one for adversity to advance upon.

Once you **realize** that everything difficult you go
　　through—every scuffed knee, lost deal, or broken
　　heart—
will eventually play wildly in your favor,
　　you'll find it hard to complain about **anything**.

Every **challenge is** an invitation to a happier place
　　than you even knew existed.

Setbacks, delays, and disappointments
　　are like steps in the mambo, tango, and cha-cha.
If you studied the movements without knowing the dance,
　　nothing would make sense.
But when you see the big picture—**poetry** in motion.

If, ever in your life, suddenly and without warning,
    an event, person, or unexpected good news
changes **everything** for the better,
    it will mean chances are astronomically **high**
. . . that it will happen again.
 And again. And again.

Words like *blame, victim,* or *fault*
    should never be used in enlightened conversations—
instead try *creator, adventurer,* or **heroine**.

Wondering how else you could view life
    when you're experiencing emotional or physical pain
is a sign of **spiritual** maturity.
    Wondering how else you could view life
when things are already going really well
    is the sign of a **spiritual rock star**.

If you aren't constantly pushing yourself to grow,
it'll mean you're **missing** something.
And that thing you're missing will eventually cause you to fall,
leading you to push yourself as you get back up,
repeating itself until you understand what you were missing.
All of which can be avoided when,
even though you think you aren't missing anything at all,
you continually **push** yourself.

You're not **meant** to bear that which you find unpleasant;
you're meant to **change** it.

Anger is almost always a sign
that you've been **quiet** for too long.
But instead of offering a solution,
it closes the mind and cools the **heart**
when both are needed most.

Usually the person you're angry at
has the most to teach you.

Not that they're **necessarily** right about
whatever you're angry about.

It won't be your cake-for-breakfast,
pajamas-in-the-afternoon,
he-loves-me kind of times
you'll remember at the end of your life
with the greatest fondness,
but your bounced-back, fears-faced,
and I-love-him kind of times.

Sometimes you have to move away, to get closer.
Let go, to stake your claim.
Be still, to move forward.
Give, to receive.
Cry, to feel the joy.
Pretend, to make it real.
Fake it, before you make it.

And sometimes, you must first decide
to feel their love, to find it was there all along.

Setbacks are only devastating
when you think they'll last forever.
They never do.

Exactly where you've been will make possible
   exactly who you become.
And one day, no matter where you've been, you'll wake up and
   feel so much joy for your life, exactly as is,
that you wouldn't trade *anything* for your past, exactly as it was . . .
   and exactly as it is on the day you read this.

The biggest misconception people have about the past
   is thinking it can detract from the rest of their lives.
To the contrary, the past only ever makes more things possible.

Although this might not make sense now,
always consider, that at the deepest level, all pain is self-inflicted.
   And when this does make sense,
      you'll find it's really great news.

Almost no one would ever choose an adventure
   if they knew they'd become hopelessly lost,
have their heart broken to pieces,
   or at times wish they'd never been born.
But absolutely everyone would choose any of those scenarios
   if they also knew that because of the chaos they'd sooner
find themselves, fall passionately in love,
   and live happily ever after.

The **only** way to find your way is to first be lost.
To make it big, start out small.
To **fall** in love, first feel none.
So, any such feelings of being lost, feeling small,
missing love, or the like should be seen as signs
that you've made a really big and daring "wish,"
and the manifestation process has **already** begun.

Of all the **joys** on earth, few compare to
the crowning glory of achieving against the odds,
succeeding in the face of peril,
or triumphing over adversity.
Yet in every such case, **without** exception,
the poor odds, peril, and adversity must come first.

Talking a lot about something that bothers you
is a pretty good sign
you've got something profoundly **liberating** to learn.

That **which** curses you today will bless you tomorrow.

That is, if you come to believe in curses and blessings
in a world where there are only **miracles.**

Said another way,

the more challenges you face on any given day,
the more happy **dancing** and **high fives** will follow.

You don't have to know how you got yourself into any mess
to know how to **move** from it.

Just because you won't always physically see life's order,
especially during crises or when disappointed,
won't mean you can't always deduce it **must** be there . . .
in absolutely insane wall-to-wall proportions.

The only **hint** you might receive
that you've begun living
the greatest chapter of your life,
is that it might start out **feeling** like the worst.

Admit, confess, and atone before you have to,
     because one day, you'll have to.
And on that day you'll realize it would have been far better
     to act and call out your **naiveté,**
than wait for the ambush.

Sadness, fear, and despair are less conditions
     than they are **decisions—**
          to see yourself as less than you really are.

When you **feel** happy, especially really happy,
     it'll seem that you've always been happy
          and that you'll **always** be happy.
Which is just as true when you feel really sad,
     lonely, depressed, broke, sick, or scared.

Which means how you **choose** to feel on any given day will
     recharacterize how you feel about your entire life.

Disappointments have little to do with circumstance
     and **everything** to do with perspective.

You can **change** how you feel in the twinkling of an eye
   if you just change what you view as important.

For whatever bothers you,
   not that it shouldn't,
know that **YOU** are the reason it bothers you.

The **reason** others might think they need you
   is because they won't yet believe they already have all that
   it takes to have all that they want.
So they **pretend** you hold the key.

And, maybe, sometimes, you might be tempted
   to **think** the same about someone else.

Practice seeing everything with spiritual eyes,
   and you'll find
. . . no predicament that can't
   be turned into an advantage,
      . . . no foe who can't become a friend, and
         . . . no burden that can't give you **wings**.

While in the pursuit of a grand and wonderful dream,
should you suddenly round a bend and see before you
an enormous uncharted mountain with towering cliffs,
jagged rocks, and seemingly impenetrable walls,
consider it a sign that your dream is far more worthwhile
than you had previously imagined.

When fear speaks, it's almost always wrong.
Unless you're being chased by wildebeests.
And when love speaks, it's almost always right.
And usually bouncy.

However wrong fear is, it often appears when you're in
exactly the right place, at exactly the right time,
doing exactly what you "should" be doing
to learn the most.

Next time you meet fear, ask,
"How might I use you and what may I learn?"

Look to what you're afraid of to learn where you can grow.

Actually, life's
    lions and tigers and bears
are really just
    angels and fairies and unicorns
that followed you here, in disguise, from worlds beyond,
    agreeing to poke, unnerve, and awaken you
whenever you forget that you're **dreaming**.

When you see things that pain you, sadden you, or make
    your heart ache, remember,
you're not seeing all.

If you think deeply enough upon those things
    that cause you great suffering and consternation,
you'll ultimately find great joy and illumination.

It really is an itty-bitty world we live on.
    And if you can maintain this perspective,
you'll be pleasantly surprised by how your challenges shrink.

The **first** step you might take
　　　toward changing unpleasant circumstances . . .
is to stop **dwelling** upon those circumstances.

The best **remedy** for dealing with a troubling past
　　　is living in the **present.**

Not on your "worst day," **during** your lowest ebb,
　　　nor through your most challenging circumstances
will you fail to **rebound** to higher heights than before.

If ever you find yourself sitting in the darkness,
　　　and then **decide** you want to sit in the light,
consider, your first few steps must be in the darkness.

Letting **go** is always easier than holding on.
　　　And it's how **new** stuff can find you faster.

It's **easier** to let go of the past once you realize that
    no matter how differently things might have gone,
you still couldn't be more **loved** than you now are,
    nor could you have more to look forward to.

Whenever there's a **genuine** commitment,
    no matter what direction you choose,
all of life's elements will align to gain you an advantage, stack
    the deck, and **prepare** one and all
for some serious legend making.

The **greater** the emotional pain,
    the greater the desire had been to **learn** the most.

Look to what's beautiful for truth.
    And to what hurts for its **beauty**.

Whenever **feeling** confused, conflicted, or bored by life,
    seek a higher perspective.
Because feeling confused, conflicted, or bored
    means **there** is one.

No matter how **things** may ever seem,
friends are always near and love is always **present.**

Nothing is ever lost.
Not time;
for what seems to have passed
lives on in the wisdom of future decisions.
Not money;
for what seems to have been spent
was only **invested.**
And not love;
for what seems to have vanished
has **only** moved so close you must look
within your heart to find it.

There is no harm, misstep, violation, or disaster
that cannot be amended, balanced, corrected, or **fixed.**

Sometimes, when it seems your wings have suddenly
and unexpectedly been clipped,
maybe, just maybe, there's **more** to learn
by **staying** where you are.

It's **often** from a sense of discontent,
feelings of incompleteness,
or even a **twinge** of true unhappiness,
that the seeds of great accomplishment
and transformation are sown.

Taking **responsibility** *doesn't mean*
you have to understand
the nuances of your role
in **bringing** about painful events,
other than acknowledging you had a role.

Nor does it mean condoning
past or present violations
or that you shouldn't defend yourself,
speak up, protest, be heard,
press **charges**, file suit,
or warn others.

Neither **does** it mean you're to blame or are at fault.

You're an ancient gladiator of love and joy who,
when choosing this lifetime, *knew what you were doing.*

Can you **imagine,** then,
considering your magnificence and zest for life,
you might **not** want to live every adventure on "easy street"?
That on occasion, if not as a rule,
you might *want to* be **challenged?**

That you might sometimes choose to be in harm's way
to spare others the pain?
That you might want to see what
you're **truly** capable of achieving and enduring?
How deeply you might love and be loved?

All under a variety of **circumstances?**

The more from your past that you accept responsibility for,
including absolutely, positively everything,
the more in your future you'll have the power to change,
including absolutely, positively **everything.**

Should you ever feel a bit bummed out and not know why
. . . or catch yourself looking back over your shoulder,
wondering . . . or sometimes asking,
What's taking so long? . . . understand,
this is typical of all spiritual overachievers.

The easiest way to avoid letdowns and disappointments
is never tricking yourself into thinking that your
happiness is dependent upon the things and events
of time and space.
Which is not to imply you can't change both.

Emotional pains are just truth knocking upon a door
that's been closed too long.

Every story has a happy ending if you believe in endings—
either in this lifetime or thereafter.
And this alone, when factoring in all of life's splendors,
will make any fleeting pain and sorrow
totally and unquestionably "worth it."

The thing that makes the darkest of times bearable,
     is **remembering** that life as you now know it,
is not reality;
     earth is simply a dreamed-up world
where **angels** earn their wings.

Meanwhile, somewhere "back home,"
     you're snug as a bug, **peacefully** sleeping
        in the palm of God's hand,
surrounded by ancient friends who can't wait for you to
     awaken and tell the stories of who and where
 you thought you were.

And once everyone has had their turn,
     you'll all look at each other mischievously,
and whisper at the same time . . .

   "Let's . . . go . . . back!"

4

imagination, **dreams,** and baby steps

Every night for countless weeks over the summer before writing this book, we fought the same battle, with varying twists. You were Moana, from our favorite Disney film. In the shallow end of our swimming pool was your invisible family; they all loved and accepted me. I was Maui (also from *Moana*). Together, we'd cross turbulent seas toward my family, on the thick blue floatie, to the deep end where the bench was built into the side of the pool, trying to elude the murderous Kakamora pirates. Shortly into our quest, the volcano mistress Te Kā (she and the pirates were also of

Moana and invisible) would rear her head, throwing massive molten lava rocks at us as we navigated to the far edge of the pool for safety. You'd scream. I'd scream. We'd fight back with all our might as the film's soundtrack blasted from patio speakers into the woods surrounding our home. Triumphant, you'd meet my family, who loved and accepted you, and we'd sail back to your family. Every night. For months.

What a production! What a summer! We were swept away by art imitating life imitating art. The magic of the ocean, so brilliantly portrayed by the writers of that great film, is exactly what I've been teaching adults, except that it works on land too. It exists for us, you're supposed to use it, it's intelligent, a friend, and it yearns to help you *help yourself.*

Implied repeatedly throughout the story was the fact that "the magic" could only help Moana when:

1. she had a dream—a specific vision, need, or goal,

2. she *really* cared, *emotionally*, about it (because she or her dream would otherwise *die*), and

3. she *first*, however feebly, took action.

Time and again she would physically throw herself into the ocean intending to save her island, or find Maui, or retrieve the emerald heart of Te Fiti. A seemingly outrageous notion that this tiny, fragile person, flung into an ocean as wide as the planet, might make a difference. Yet because she did act, demonstrating belief and expectation, *the*

ocean responded. Came alive. And exponentially magnified her efforts.

This is life's greatest manifesting secret, after passionately having a dream and caring about it, *you must act on it, even when you don't know what to do.* Even when it seems hopeless. Even when you don't know how your mortal "baby steps" could possibly make a difference.

Having a goal is easy. Caring about it is usually easy too. But taking action when it feels like your chances of success are infinitesimal—that takes a superhero. Only when you act does life's magic respond. You've got to have skin in the game, or there's no game. Do something, literally anything in the vague direction of your dream, *regularly and consistently,* and then, seemingly from nowhere, when you least expect, the magical winds of change begin to howl.

When the pool got too cold to swim in, your imagination would soar indoors. Some nights at bath time you were a rainbow kitty, colors revealed as if by magic once you were in the water. Other evenings we'd grab the kiddie paint and transform the aluminum ladder in the garage into an ever more beautiful pink, flowered staircase. To where? I didn't ask, because really, once you have a pink, flowered staircase, does it matter where it leads?

These were your stories, I was just the lucky guy who landed a co-starring role in the productions. And as I marvel now at our Academy Award–worthy performances, I'm rather amazed to realize that probably 97 percent of our adventures took place in our minds. I'm further wowed thinking that this ratio never changes throughout our life, no matter our age, no matter what we do.

What we want, what we fear, what we dream of, how we prepare, how we react, what we endure, what we decide, is almost *all* mental. Even if you're physically engaged in rigorous performances all day, every day, the mental planning, preparation, and evolving drama is still at least 97 percent of your experience . . . by my admittedly not-remotely-scientific-certainly-underestimated measure. Right?

So, here's my offer. With life's *inner game* mastered early on, the rest of your life, the tiny part that shows up in time and space, will be a crazy-easy downhill slide. Perfecting your imagination to dream, to engage, to pretend, and to act. Sparking passion to inspire and ramp up a heightened sense of anticipation. Ultimately cultivating enough confidence that you believe in yourself and your journey, enabling resilience and patience, creating every opportunity for life's magic to reach and transform you.

Imagination *is* life. And yours will serve you well as you grow up—*especially when you know what you're doing.* Which is sure to happen if you stay true to yourself and you learn to tune out the voices that would strip you of believing in magic, make-believe, and the power of pretending. Keep your invisible friends. Be unpredictable. A tad unreasonable. Spontaneous. A dreamer.

Pay no attention to those who say life is hard. That we're here to be tested. That success is about survival of the fittest, hard work, and lucky breaks. That opportunity only knocks once. The early bird gets the worm. No matter how much those who say these things care about you.

Fortunately, the truth is a hard thing to lose. People, with all that they fear and all the limits they believe in, are still "irrationally" full of optimism. Fables and folklore insist that dreams come true, science now tells us that there's an energy to positive thinking, athletes are encouraged to visualize, in *The Secret* we talked about it as a universal law of attraction, and I've been telling people for 20 years that our thoughts *literally* become the things and events of our lives.

To repeat one of the most important lessons in this book, "thinking" is where and how you fit into the equation of reality creation. Learning how to "aim that thing" and calculating engagement is what this chapter is about. It's an add-on to chapter 2, with more specificity about the subtle art of breathing life into your dreams.

Imagine . . .

87

Time and space is where we chase things
    we **pretend** we don't have—
love, friends, and abundance—
    while worrying about things we pretend we do have—
problems, challenges, and issues.
    Until one day we **happen** to notice
the prophetic powers of pretending.

To **build** a mansion in time and space,
    whether of mortar, gold, or friendships,
think of imagination as your blueprint,
    desire as your **funding,**
faith as your builder, and action
    as proof these dots are being connected.

Treating any old job as if it were your dream job
    is the fastest way to spark the kind of life changes
that will yield your dream **job.**

Same for any old house, friend, **day,** life,
    or **pair** of espadrilles.

Great **big,** ear-to-ear, open-mouth smiles
  are responsible for far more sizzling romances,
salary increases, life extensions, and calorie burning
  than our dentists, doctors, and financial planners
  will ever **comprehend.**

Smiling or laughing for no reason at all
  is one of the best reasons to smile or laugh—
plus, **doing** either will summon circumstances
  that will give you reason after reason.

Bringing new things into your life boils down to
  learning to think of **yourself** with them.
And vice versa for removing things from your life.

Always speak of the past gratefully.
  Of the future, excitedly.
And of the present, with **bobbing** eyebrows
  and a Cheshire grin.

If anyone should ever ask if you're enlightened . . .
    always say, "Yes!"
Same if they ask whether or not you're healthy,
    wealthy, and loved **beyond** imagination.

When in **doubt**, show up early, think less, feel more,
    ask once, give thanks, **expect** the best,
appreciate everything, never give up, make it fun, lead,
    invent, regroup, wink, chill, smile,
and live as if your success were **inevitable,**
    and so it shall be.

Every fortune, comeback, or kiss
    was first a thought, a **whisper,** a dream.

The trick with imagination is remembering to use it.

Creative visualization, as an exercise,
    gives the biggest bang for the least effort.
Visualize, every weekday (you can take weekends off),
        no longer than a few minutes,
imagine your dreamed-of end results,
    as if they'd already come to pass,
        fueled by emotion,
                yourself in the picture,
                    smiling broadly,
        happy tears running down your face.

If you're at least visualizing or meditating enough
    to wonder whether or not you're doing it right,
you're doing it right
    and you're way ahead of the game.

The secret to living the life of your dreams is
    to start living them at once, however humbly,
        to any degree you can.
If you can't travel far, travel near.
    If you can't dine out, go for dessert.
If you don't have a travel partner, be your own.

The secret to **performing** miracles lies in:
    1. Knowing your desired outcome.
        2. *Not* knowing how you'll pull it off.
          3. **Proceeding** anyway.

Should you ever be in need of a miracle,
    think not of the miracle, not even a little,
but instead of its intended **result.**

Little **ducks** never line up until momma duck just goes—
    the same will be **true** of getting your ducks in a row.

Rarely are the first **steps** in a journey anything like the
    final ones, either in direction, pace, or grace.
Which means that none of those **things** are even half as
    important as the fact that there are steps at all.

Usually, if you just start **"dancing,"** the "music" will
    be added—as will the partners, a giant disco ball,
        and **whatever** else you need.
Because the resources you need to complete a **journey**
    are only added once you begin it.

The **odd** thing about inspiration is
that it usually comes **after**, not before,
a new journey is **started**.

When **just** starting out on a new journey,
it's only natural to feel vulnerable.
After all it may seem that you have much to lose.
The **truth**, however, is that never again
at any other point in the same journey
will you have so much to gain.

Don't let the dazzling **heights** you aspire
to scare you from getting started.
Few could climb Mount Everest tomorrow,
though virtually all could **begin** preparing.

It's more **important** to start,
than to start in the **right** direction.

There's **nothing** you've ever done
    that wasn't significantly done for you,
      once you got **started.**
Remember that next time you're overwhelmed
    at the outset of a new adventure.

Most **big** ideas don't seem like big ideas at first.
    So, be on the lookout for little ones that seem kind of
ho-hum, let-me-floss-first kind of **ideas.**

Until the **really** great stuff comes along,
    do the not-so-great stuff,
because for those who dream big, the not-so-great stuff
    always leads to the really **great** stuff.

Great **big** innovative, world-changing ideas are plentiful.
    People who take tiny little baby steps **toward** them
      are rare.

It's okay to dream big and start small—
    you'll probably **have** to.

The **real** reason so many have trouble with taking baby steps
is because they think those steps are
important for the distance covered.
Not realizing that each one **triggers** enormous leaps
and bounds taken on their behalf in realms unseen.

Life's magic isn't a substitute for networking,
socializing, preparing, or cold calling.
To the contrary, these are some of its **greatest** incubators.

Don't be **afraid** to do the obvious.
Not all miracles hide in the unseen.
Some hang around, **waiting** for you to call,
write, or show up.

It's better to have loved and lost,
tried and failed, dreamed and missed,
than to sit out your turn in fear.
Because the loss, the failure, and the miss are only temporary,
whereas the love, the **adventure,** and the dream
will never stop paying dividends.

You simply can't lose something
      you're still capable of giving.
You can't fail if you haven't stopped trying.
        And you can't miss if you're still aiming.

The thing that most forget, while dreamily looking off
      into the horizon for the ship of their dreams,
is that such ships never sail in,
      but are built beneath our very feet.

Here's a little "Inevitability Test" to check on the progress
      you're making toward achieving any particular dream:

You're pretty much doing something about it every single day.

Consistent effort, no matter how small,
      sparks magic, fills sails, butters bread, turns tides,
instills faith, summons friends, improves health,
      burns calories, creates abundance, yields clarity,
builds courage, spins planets, and rewrites destinies.

Opportunity never stops knocking.
   And neither should you.

There are more than enough worms for every bird,
      early and late.
What matters is that you keep showing up.

Thinking big but acting small
      is the same as thinking small.

It's not the size of your dreams that determines
      whether they come true,
but the size of the actions you take
      that imply their inevitable arrival.

Sometimes the hard way is really the easy way
      and the slow way is really the fast way.
Yet such sublime surprises may remain
      forever unknown if you just wait for the
quick and easy way.

Practice. Study. Prepare yourself.
Think. Act. Face your beasts.
Pay the piper whatever dues you think you have to pay.
Do the **dance,** walk the fire, wait in line.
Plant the seeds, hoe the field, go to market.
Because on the day that you become
all that you may ever **dream** of becoming,
there's simply no price you'd find too great.

The **anticipated** happiness
that moves you in the direction
of a new dream will **always** pale in comparison to the
actual happiness you'll find once it comes **true.**
Which is **worth** trying to imagine, anyway.

The more you **push** yourself into areas of discomfort—
gently, just a bit, from time to time—
the more "comfortable" you'll become in those areas.

The **opposite** is also true.

Do not abandon the **tools** of intellect,
    logic, and common sense,
but combine them with your feelings, **faith**,
    and imagination.

Avoiding something draws it ever near.
    Defending yourself can become a full-time job.
And worrying about things that **might** never happen
    increases their chances of happening.

Never forget that all you may ever dream of having
    is far less than what you **already** have.

Manifesting deadlines are fine
    when **placed** upon yourself,
like "write a new chapter every month," as guides or goals,
    but don't give **deadlines** to the Universe and its magic,
like, "Have a publisher by year-end."
    You simply cannot see enough of your dream's required
logistics, in relation to all of your other desires,
    and in relation to those of the world,
to do so **effectively** without risking limitation
    or sacrificing other dreams.

The **greatest** trick and most subtle secret
    to doing anything really, **really** well
is loving that you get to do it at all.

Do it **your** way, that's why you're here.

The **presumption**, at all times
    and under all circumstances, should always be that
you are good enough, worthy enough, and lovable enough.
    And that you are exactly the **right** kind of person,
in the right place, at the right time to have the life you want.
    Otherwise, you wouldn't have been given
such dreams to begin with.

Sometimes **you'll** learn much more about life,
    love, and happiness,
    – when you're single than when you're in a relationship,
  – when you're **looking** for work than when you're working,
        and
    – when you're confused rather than when you're clear
    . . .

. . . which doesn't mean don't seek change
   if you want there to be **change.**
It means, if you can allow yourself to learn what there is
   to **learn,** from wherever you now are,
      rather than resist,
you'll greatly accelerate your **dreamed** of transformation.

When you don't know what to do next,
   it might be because you've **already** done more than
you **give** yourself credit for,
   and it's time to chill out a bit.

Very **often** when you just can't decide between two
   or more options,
the answer that would give you the most peace
   . . . hasn't **yet** arrived.

Ask, yet expect.
   Surrender, yet prepare.
And **miracles** will abound.

The **only** way to get what you really want
    is to know what you really want.
And the only way to know what you really want
    is to **know** yourself.
And the only way to know yourself is to be yourself.
And the only way to be yourself is to
    listen to your **heart.**

Enjoying short-term pleasures
    to the detriment of long-term dreams
is as crazy as **pursuing** long-term dreams
    to the detriment of short-term pleasures.
Both are important.

Impatience is a sign that you've temporarily forgotten
    to behave at all times as if your dreams
    have **already** come true.

The more you **hurry,** the slower you go.
    The more you wait, the **longer** it takes.

It's **totally** possible to have big, huge, gigantic dreams,
yet still be deliriously **happy** before they come true.

Sometimes, when things take longer
                    than you thought they would,
it's just a reminder from your **higher** self that you have
            more time than you thought and that
there's a journey to enjoy.

The **shortest** distance between here and there—
        or between today and the life of your wildest dreams—
        runs through **joy.** Be led by it

When you **hang** out in time and space long enough,
        you'll inevitably learn it's through the twin gateways of
persistence and **patience** that masters become masters.

Persistence is priceless,
        but its value lies in doing, doing, **doing,**
not in waiting, waiting, waiting.
Not knocking on one door until it opens,
        but knocking on **all** of them until one opens.

Whenever **spending** or investing,
    whether a little or a lot, wisely or not,
remember to celebrate that you're creating **opportunities,**
    exchanging energy, dancing with life,
      supporting economies, feeding families,
    lessening poverty, demonstrating courage,
validating others, eradicating fear, inviting magic,
    and lifting humanity higher into the **light.**

Actually, **creating** wealth is even more fun than spending it,
    so be sure to daydream as much about the former
                as the **latter.**

The best way to **manifest** money,
    which is just as true for manifesting love,
is to focus less on these by-products of a life well lived
    and more on a life well **lived.**

It's not **thinking** about the bucks that makes one rich,
    but thinking rich that **makes** the bucks.

It takes a really **special** person to find true happiness
in the lap of luxury, surrounded by friends
and laughter, and choices, choices, choices.
And oddly, it's **usually** the exact same kind of person
who could have been equally happy without all that,
spending time alone, **maybe** with a book,
or some tools, or a dog.

The **self-made** millionaire invariably
thinks about income **more** than expenses.
And probably about customers, more than vendors;
possibilities more than risks;
smiles more than frowns;
options more than commitments;
vacations more than overtime;
detours more than setbacks;
opportunities more than obstacles.

It's **okay** to love material things;
matter is pure spirit, only more so,
because you've thought about it so much,
you've **brought** it to "life."

The most **surefire** way to find yourself,
    make a friend,
        turn a buck,
            and **discover** your power
is to help someone else do the **same.**

One of the most advanced forms of self-help
    is **helping** others.
So please, when in doubt or when in trouble,
    "help **yourself.**"

True selfishness is
    honoring God's unique expression in you,
which will ensure that as the winds of divinity
    are blown through your **heart,**
the melody is unlike any other.

To **care** for self *at the expense* of others
    is not selfishness, but ignorance.
We all depend to some degree upon the **whole** to truly
    prosper, and when any one of us suffers, all suffer.

Living deliberately starts with imagining your dreams
as if they have already come true.
It's a matter of switching gears, never looking back, and
being the person that you've always dreamed you'd be.
Predicating your behavior on *their* reality,
not the old illusions that will still surround you.

Living your life from *their* mind-set.
Entertaining every thought, saying every word,
and making every decision from *their* point of view.
Walking the way they would walk,
dressing the way they would dress,
and spending your free time
the way they would spend theirs.

Frequently, in time and space, right before a really
HUGE dream comes true
. . . nothing seems to be happening.

So if, perchance, it ever appears as if
absolutely nothing is happening in your life,
particularly after you've been dreaming big and taking
action . . . consider it . . .

a sign.

Probably the **most** important thing I could tell you
about living the life of **your** dreams,
would be to point out that you **already** are.

5

making the
most
of friends, family
& relationships

You won't remember this, you were two. We were at the kids' park playing follow the leader, each of us jostling to be at the front of our two-person conga line, when a little boy about your size walked into our space, causing us to stop while you stared at him, then at me, then at him, before asking in a hopeful tone without malice, "Daddy, can you make him disappear?"

And then there was the time, at the same park a few months later, when you timidly drifted from me toward the two slightly older girls sitting and chattering away in the

sand-filled, vacated volleyball court with dolls and shovels. I watched as you approached, eyebrows raised, in your first self-chosen social encounter of your own creation, about to connect with new best friends formulating the most magical words you could imagine to greet them, probably, "My name is Rebecca. That's my daddy," as was your go-to self-identifying phrase around strangers . . . when suddenly, as if these two you approached were cleverly disguised samurai sword–carrying ninja warriors, with the spin of her head toward you, the leader cleaved you in half, pronouncing you unworthy: *"No. Not here. GO!"* Shredding your heart and mine with her unceremonious words. Her execution was so abrupt, I fleetingly hoped you didn't understand, except the command was punctuated with a snap of her extended arm and pointed finger telling you exactly which way to depart.

Frozen in shock and grief, your fragile smile replaced by a grimaced awkwardness, unable to step in any direction, the building anguish so great you couldn't speak your name or even cry to me, tears welling as you tried to maintain your composure, I saw you die in defeat. Until you did cry, uncontrollably, withering into my fast-approaching arms. Your pain was deep. Heartbroken. Confused. Sad. Suffering. Devastated. And utterly inconsolable.

I tried to tell you it didn't matter, that they were not being nice, that they were unworthy of your interest, that there were other, more fun things for us to do. That life was still beautiful, the sun was still shining, the day was not done . . . but you couldn't hear me. I frantically wondered what else I could do to minimize the crippling memory and lasting scar of this fateful day . . .

Fifteen minutes later you were fine. *What?*

I wonder, though, if you'll have the same recovery time when you're 15? 25? Older? With *understanding*, it could be the same—If you'd even allow yourself to feel so hurt by the fickle behavior of others in the first place. Because with understanding you'd know to rely on yourself for approval. You'd find that what others say and do reflects their issues, not yours. And you'd learn that you are more than what happens on any step of your life's path; you are more, even, than the path itself. With understanding you'll better be able to see yourself *as I now see you*, which will remind you always of how deeply you're loved.

Little will add to your life as much as your relationships, although what you gain, when, how, and with who, won't always be as predictable as you'd like, nor will your gains necessarily coincide with what you hoped to be receiving. And little else will build you up as much or tear you down as quickly as what you learn from love. Until, in the end, with a heart that learns to be open and vulnerable, you'll find that it was you, all along, who did the building and tearing.

Not that others won't have a role, given by you, to assist in your "construction." And conversely, you'll often be granted roles in helping to shape the lives of others. Understand, however, that no one can come into our lives who's not preapproved. Their probable actions and behaviors known in advance of whenever your paths may cross.

Which is to say, that while you're the ultimate authority of what happens in your life, one of your more clever levers for effecting this, will be who you draw or allow into your adventure, and what behaviors you help to elicit from them through your own thoughts, words, and deeds.

Sounds complicated, but it's not. All you need to take from this, is that those in your life are "on board" with your manifestations and lessons, present and future, just as you are for theirs. True teammates. Love bound, however you may fumble or offend. Your needs, fears, and passions are intertwined. Compatible. Complementary. Today. Tomorrow . . . minds may change.

In this chapter I'll share what I've learned in my life on love, rejection, longing, sharing, disappointment, compromise, commitment, and moving on. But no matter how much I may open your heart to the little I know about love, you will still, for the rest of your life, persistently desire to have certain people appear in, or disappear from, yours, and to have them otherwise behave in certain preferable ways. They will have similar wishes of you.

Throughout, remember who you really are to each other. Kindred spirits drawn together in the romantic adventure of life. Fellow actors lost in these illusions to learn what's true and real. Honor each other. Enjoy the camaraderie. Treat one another with the same kindness and respect you hope to be afforded. Understand that just as others might hurt you out of confusion, so will you them. And as much as you'd like to hear apologies or to be forgiven, so would they.

In the meantime, no matter who else comes or goes from your adventure, please know I'll *always* be there, in one form or another, to catch you when you fall, send angels when you call, and love you through it all.

You're simply the greatest.

you are loved

If **everyone** really knew how much they were loved,
    not only from **"above,"**
        but by those now in their life,
there'd be **little** hearts drawn on everything
    from wheelbarrows to skyscrapers to jumbo jets.

When something **hurts** your eyes, stop looking at it.
    When it hurts your ears, **stop** listening to it.
And when it hurts your heart, stop **justifying** it.

In the **beginning,** the price of giving great love
    is risking that it won't be returned.
In the end, however, you'll find great love
    is always **returned.**

To **err** on the side of generosity, patience,
    love, or **kindness** is not to err.

If you could **actually** stand in someone else's shoes
    to hear what they hear, see what they see,
and feel what they feel, you would **honestly** wonder what
    planet they live on
and be blown away by how different their
    "reality" is from yours.

You'd also never, in a million years, be quick to judge again.

Being happy without a partner
    is the fastest way to attract one.
            If you even want one.

One of **love's** many corollaries is that the brighter your
    light, the more you attract . . . **everything.**
            Moths and butterflies.
At which **point** you begin learning what to celebrate
    and what to let **fly** on by.

There is no such thing as an **ideal** relationship status,
    except yours, today, for now.

�֍

Of **all** the reasons you might draw someone into your life,
one would never be to **find** their faults.

✖

Putting up your defenses will inspire others
to put up their **offenses.**

✖

Sometimes it may **help** to see difficult people
as reminders of what you may have put **others** through.
Or to see grouchy people as those who may have chosen
a more challenging life than you.

✖

When you look for what's **right**—in others,
in relationships, in yourself, and in your journey—
you'll always **find** it.

Same when you look for what's **wrong.**

✖

You may not ever understand what's going on in
"their" life,
but you can always figure out what's going on in yours.
Let their shortcomings inspire you
to work on your own.

Sometimes, the person whose life looks the easiest
has had it the hardest,
but they're really good at not dwelling on the past,
living in the moment,
having dreams for tomorrow,
and "rolling like that."

Always, the strong carry the weak,
the rich carry the poor, the healthy carry the sick,
and the happy carry the sad.

And it's probably because this was once their promise,
to thank those who earlier carried them.

Everyone gets carried a little bit, which is something
to remember when it's your turn to carry.

Seeing things from someone else's **perspective**
    can totally **change** your life.
Which might even explain why they're in yours
    to begin with.

In your **times** with others you'll laugh and cry,
    and in your times alone you'll understand why—
    let there be **both.**

Arguments are won intellectually, **not** love.

Being fair and reasonable
    will earn you respect and admiration,
but being genuinely **kind**
    will make you a total love **magnet.**

Ask with love
    and their answer may surprise you.

Hear with **love** and your answer may surprise them.

⋇

Simply **dwelling** upon joy, abundance,
    or anything else that might involve other people
will literally draw complete strangers into your life who
    will **bring** those things,
when in alignment with all else you dwell upon.

⋇

At all times and in all places, be the **first** to smile.

⋇

While it's often **fashionable**
    to dwell upon what might have been,
what's usually not **understood** is that,
    really and truly, it couldn't have.

Most of the time when people think the present could
    have been **different** than it is,
it's because they think the past was different than it was.

Be **glad** things went as they did—you still have forever.

⋇

When someone **treats** you differently than you expected,
   it's usually because you've **been**
sending out **mixed** signals.

No matter what you do that may disappoint or hurt others,
   always keep in mind, it was the very best you could
have done, with what you **knew** at the time.

And so will this be **true** of others
   who disappoint or hurt **you.**

When it comes to **choosing** who will be in your life,
   be sure to value their *"Cowabunga!"*
quality as much as all others.

The more it seems **"love hurts,"**
   the more you can be sure it's something else,
like pride, fear, or not remembering
   how **fabulous** you are.

Those in **great** relationships aren't always those
who are good at relationships.
And those in **challenging** relationships
aren't always those who are bad at relationships.

No matter how great the **desire** is to please another,
let it be no greater than the desire to **be** yourself.

Don't **trust** anyone who tells you your happiness is more
important to them than their **own**.

When you **finally** see what this whole
time-space thing is all about,
you're going to laugh; you're going to cry;
and you're going to be so very **grateful**
you LOVED as much as you did.

There's nothing **unspiritual**
about ending a relationship, for any reason
or for no reason, so long as you do it with **love**.

No one **owes** anyone anything.
     No matter who they are. No matter what they've done.
No matter how **much** they may claim
     to suffer without you.

Those who **deserve** your love the least
     are usually the ones who need it the **most**.

Some, however, are better loved at a **distance**.
     For a while, anyway.
Fortunately, **love** doesn't really know the difference.

The **lower** the price of your love, the higher its value;
     the fewer the conditions, the **greater** its reach.

The criteria for **unleashing** torrents
     of love upon thine enemy
lies first in knowing that there should be no **criteria**.

❧

When love is otherwise hard to feel for someone,
allow it to **begin** with sympathy.

❧

Your "soul mate" might not be the same person
throughout your life,
and sometimes it **might** just be you.

❧

Only do those things you **want** to do,
with **whom** you want to do them.

❧

Always **follow** your heart,
unless it's been **broken.**
Then you must lead it.
Back into love.

❧

Hearts are never too big to mend,
too small to rebound,
or too tired to love **again.**

When the **choice** is to hurt or be hurt,
     cheat or be cheated, violate or be violated,
always, always, **always** choose the latter.
     And then try to figure out how you created such
a fork in the road of your **life** to begin with.

Always, kindness prevails—
     no matter how things **appear,**
nor how humbling a task, nor how **unkind** they've been.

When someone **speaks** on a topic unfamiliar to you,
     you might be able to gauge the **honesty** and accuracy
of their words by all else they've ever shared with **you**
     on topics you were familiar with.

Same **for** authors.

Sometimes, **expecting** a straight answer from some
     people is absolutely out of the question.
Which should answer your **question.**

It's **always** best to assume that everyone either
knows the truth, or will know the **truth,**
because they either do or they will.

When you **understand** that your disappointment in
another's behavior always stems from
their immaturity, or **yours,**
rather than their unkindness, or yours,
it becomes much harder not to keep **skipping** through
life, giddy with joy, smelling the flowers.

When someone **behaves** poorly, it's always because
they've forgotten how **powerful** they really are,
how **beautiful** life is, or how much they're loved.

At this **very** moment there are people only you can reach.
Some of whom may have chosen this very **lifetime**
hoping you'd be in theirs.

The best way to **deal** with other people . . .
    is to just let them be **other** people.

One of the most **helpful** things you can do
    for another is to let them
learn their lessons for **themselves,**
    at their own pace.
It's **also** one of the most helpful things
    you can do for **yourself.**

The **only** person who should ever have to live by your
    standards, is **you.**
Let everyone else off the hook.

The most **effective** way of changing another person,
    though not guaranteed,
comes from changing how **you** see them.

If you **don't** really *have to* change someone
     to keep on loving them, then don't.
Because trying to **change** one thing about them
     might change **other** things about them.

For as **long** as you wish to **keep** someone in your life,
     whoever they may be,
understanding them, as opposed to changing them,
     will wildly improve **chances**
they'll wish to keep you in their life.

How you treat **people,** in general,
     is the single biggest factor for determining
how people, in general, will **treat** you.

This does not always work, however,
     in **one-on-one** relationships.

Expecting and *preparing* for someone's very best behavior—
     in **terms** of respect, kindness, love,
or just winning their attention—guarantees nothing.
     But wildly improves your chance of **receiving** it . . .

. . . better, if you don't **insist** that such behavior
come from a specific **person,**
chances of receiving it from someone else "as good or better,"
at the right time, are 100 **percent.**

Nothing you might ever do
can ensure anyone **else's** happiness.

It's **not** that people will act a **certain** way around you,
but that you'll attract certain **types** of people and
behaviors based upon your thoughts, beliefs,
and **expectations** of them.

When you change, the people you attract
and their **behaviors** will change.

A **kind** word can move mountains and change lives.
But for those times when they **escape** you,
when the right thing isn't said, or the time wasn't right to say it,
kind **thoughts** can do the same.

Thoughts have a way of lingering, seeking, and **finding**
their intended beneficiary, unfettered by time and space.

Your **kind** thoughts and deeds toward others—
    like sharing a smile, a compliment, or a helping hand—
plant seeds of beauty, **hope,** and love that will one day grow
    into a spectacular garden that *you* will get to call **home.**

Forgiveness is **only** necessary when first there's blame.
    And blame can only be **cast**
            when first there's misunderstanding.

    Better to accept that at some level, for some reason,
you chose to participate in whatever happened between
    you and someone else, and thereby reclaim your **power,**
than to abdicate responsibility through a false belief
    that bad things can happen to good people,
            setting yourself up for another fall.

As is true of **kissing,**
    let your life know both spontaneity and thoughtfulness.

Sexual orientation is like being left- or right-handed—
    it's not random, it will serve you,
and you are far, far more than any orientation.

Good looks have less to do with one's body
    and more to do with one's mind.

Looks change, beauty lasts.

Sometimes, more can be learned
    from the disagreeable
than the agreeable.

Any profound difference you make
    in the life of someone else will always be smaller
than the difference it will make in your own.

Success is better measured in smiles received,
      giggles heard, and hands held
   than in dollars earned, deadlines met, and weight lost.

Know everyone by their good traits.

Sometimes, it's not just about finding the perfect
            friend, partner, or tribe,
but finding the perfection in those you've already found.

See everyone you meet as a brand-new chance to fall in love
      for a different reason than ever before.

Friends are friends because they've discovered
      how much they have in common.
Enemies are friends too,
      who've not yet discovered this.

For **anyone**, ever, to be in your life,
    you have something to **gain.** Besides their absence.

Although your **acquiring** the self-confidence to say,
"I love you, good-bye," might be a reason.

If you can see the little girl or little boy in another,
    you'll probably **find** that the mask they wear
isn't to inspire your fear, but to **hide** their own.

Sometimes, **understanding** their fears, helps you to
    understand their pain and their behavior.
And understanding their **fears** sometimes helps you to
    understand your own.

The next time someone upsets you, think to yourself,
Thanks for pointing out that I've begun depending on you.

And the next time someone doesn't take your view into account, think,
That's okay, I was once like that.

And if someone steals from you, think,
It was nothing, my supply is the Universe . . .

. . . or lies to you, think,
I'm sorry you feel that need.

Violates you,
All for my growth and glory.

Is rude to you,
Cheer up, dear soul, it'll be okay.

Judges you,
Thanks for sharing.

Drives by you like a bat out of hell,
Be careful, my friend, you are loved.

And the next time someone greets you with a smile, smile back, like you're sharing a great secret.

The great thing about feeling **deep,**
  earthshaking love . . .
    is that you can start with anyone.

Send them **love.**
  Wish them peace. See them **happy.**

Everyone, always, forever.

6

what
old souls
know

Dream.

I'm not an "old soul," but you might be. It's an expression, of course, that universally means a kinder person, typically more patient, thoughtful and wise than most, presumably from lots of earthly experience. Perhaps, some speculate, experience that spans many lifetimes.

It's harder to know the soul age of kids because you were all so recently on the other side, "closer" to Source, from which we all emerged. Your worldview is less complicated than grown-ups'. I remember my niece, your cousin, when your age—upon learning of death and giving it some thought—suddenly blurted out, "Mommy, I know what happens when we die!"

"What, honey? What happens when we die?"

"We go back to normal."

We're a *long way* from normal right now. But imagine, as I've already shared, it was from "normal" that we chose to come here. In our existence prior to entering the illusions, as the God-particles we had to have been, in pure radiance and light. Even from here we can deduce that back then we had to have been pretty amazing, in all of our glory, everywhere, always, at once, with thoughts that spontaneously changed everything, showered in love and knowing it, metaphorically in the palm of God's hand. *Pure* God, ourselves. There's only one thing that could rival that, make it better, even, exploding all possibilities into even more possibilities . . . *voluntarily losing ourselves to be here.* On one condition, of course: Our return to "normal" must be guaranteed. Otherwise, who would ever leave?

My little brain cannot conceive of anything, in all creation, not in any sphere of existence, that might be as audacious and brilliant as being born into time and space without any recollection of our divinity. Having to find our own way when lost, our own courage when frightened, and the infinite powers at our disposal when challenged. Left to the elements to rediscover our supremacy over them. Driven by our passions so that we might rise above our humble, naked beginnings and ultimately see through the illusions that have hypnotized us.

136

Only to find ourselves once again high upon the throne of "thy kingdom come" (used to be a Catholic, loved the pageantry), from whence it all began.

The deepest truth, of course, is that we never left our throne or stopped being pure God. *Not remembering this*, however, is the kicker that has made our adventures possible.

I want you to start remembering.

You have your work cut out for you. To give some context to the times you've landed in, taken as a whole, I'd say the soul age of the world today is still quite young, comparable to an individual in his or her late teenage years learning about responsibility and consequence. Easy to judge by simply observing our collective behavior.

Obviously, we're in a precarious orbit. At a critical point in shaping our destiny, which hinges entirely on the private and collective decisions we make that increasingly have global implications. Of course, we knew what we were getting into, born when we were, that the world would be moving from darkness into the light, from confusion and fear into truth and love; that we'd be alive at the dawn of our species' spiritual awakening. And you, born when you were, knew, given our natural propensity to self-correct and thrive, there'd still be a great likelihood of stunning advances in every field of humanity during this very lifetime.

Knowing this will hopefully ground and reassure you. What matters most, however, are *your* choices in this lifetime, not who you were and what you did in others. Facing today's fears. Living today's dreams. Creating new stories.

Understanding yourself. The lessons that follow in this chapter are meant to move you to those ends, as I aim to whittle down the list of questions you might still have.

These observations and conclusions were arrived at in the same way as the earlier chapters, through blending experience, logic, and intuition. I've found throughout my life that by holding on to questions long enough, particularly ones that doubled me over in angst or awe, the answers I sought inevitably arrived. Here, again, my ideas are not unique; you'd arrive at them on your own should you have the interest, yet to offer you a boost so that you might peer from "my shoulders," perhaps even into realms I cannot yet see, I humbly continue.

Good God almighty.

In all **battles** between the heart and mind,
    go with your **heart.**
For truly, it's a lot easier for your mind
    to catch up with your heart,
than for your heart to catch up with your **mind.**

Step one for **changing** the entire world is
    falling in love with it as it **already** is.

Same for changing yourself.

Sometimes a **lack** of clarity,
    is actually the clarity you were in **need** of.

The **older** the soul, the softer the glance,
    the quicker the **smile,** and the sooner to **say,**
        "I love you."

They also tend to hold hands with those they walk beside.

When **pondering** the vastness of the cosmos,
    keep in mind that it goes even farther **inward**
than outward.

You can **usually** tell an old soul
    by how indifferent they are to setbacks
and by how **friendly** they are to trees.

Young souls use pain to learn how things are.
    Mature souls use pain to learn
              how **else** things might be.
And **old** souls use pain to learn how else they might be.

Random **awkwardness**, unexpected shyness,
    feared inadequacy, and occasional blushing
are just a few **signs** that a
    giant is settling into their **greatness.**

Always **listen** to your doubts.

Not just because they might **teach** you of your fears
    but because, sometimes, they might teach you
        of your **wisdom.**

Those who say, "I don't know what to do,"
   usually do know what to do.

Disappointment without anger is the mark of an old soul.

Not being disappointed is the mark of a really old soul.

And trusting life so thoroughly
   that every step on its path is valued
more than where it was supposed to take you,
   is the mark of eternal youth.

Of all the things that really and truly matter,
   working efficiently and getting more done
is not among them.

The day will come, if it hasn't already,
   when nothing else will matter to you as much
as helping others to succeed and to find the happiness
   you have found.

You only have to **ride** the wave of life,
        not **create** it.

Nine out of ten old souls **agree** that one of
        the very best things about spiritual maturity
is appreciating that age is so very meaningless.

The tenth soul?
        Out **climbing** trees and couldn't be reached.

The best way to **create** more free time,
        is to **take** it.

To move a **mountain,**
        befriend it, him, or her.

Everything that's ever **happened** to you,
        up until reading these very words,
was just practice for the really **good** stuff that's to follow.

Each **blossom** still blooms in its field,
    each child still clutches your hand,
        and each friend still lingers in your **heart**.
Just because a window of **time** has closed
    doesn't mean what it showed you is gone.

You needn't be **intimidated** by your dreams
        or scared by your fears,
because in a world of illusion, where you are **their** creator,
        you are also their **greater**.

When **driving** down the road of life,
    rarely do you know how **good** you have it,
        until you see it in the rearview mirror.
Unless you **remember** this mid-drive,
        which should be right about **now**.

Young **souls** look to secrets, rites, and rituals.
    Mature souls look to science, math, and evidence.
And old souls just look **within**.

The **pursuit** of money as a means to anything
    should always be secondary
to the pursuit of the thing itself.

The sun asks not that the moon and planets
    help **brighten** each day
but relishes her role as a **keeper** of the light
    and a bringer of the dawn.
A role, no doubt, that will be much like **your** own.

Some **people** bloom late. Some very late.
    And some, very, very late. But, they all **bloom.**
And the **longer** it takes, the more spectacular it is.

Dimming your **light** in sadness or empathy
    over the suffering of others **doesn't** help anyone.

Sometimes it's your downtime,
   lounging-in-bed-too-long time, walkabout time,
watching-the-rain time and blow-Friday-off time
      that makes possible your greatest achievements.

When you give yourself permission
   to be totally unproductive,
      and you actually relish such interludes,
your genius, creativity, and productivity
         will increase exponentially.

A sign that you're approaching enlightenment,
   beyond auras, ringing bells, and a healing touch,
is that you start valuing idle daydreaming
   as much as you value being in the throes of creativity.

And that you begin talking sweetly, not only to plants
   and trees, but to cars and toasters and computers.

You find you're eagerly picking up trash in public places.

And, quite unequivocally, you begin to feel gratitude for
   present challenges, love for lousy drivers,
and sympathy for those who don't see service in their work.

   Until you arrive, then, these might be ways to lean in.

It's **perfectly** okay, and sometimes highly ideal,
    to claim all is well amid doubt and confusion.
To be happy in spite of challenges. To **laugh** at problems.
    Dance without a partner. Sing without a rhyme.
And talk to inanimate **objects.**

You might be an old soul when, in spite of the usual challenges,
    you'd be **happy** to live another 10,000 lifetimes,
        even though your learning is almost done.
Whereas feeling impatience or **boredom**
    usually means you've got more living to do.

While you **may,** from time to time, envy others, it's precisely
    during those moments when you might ask yourself
whether or not you'd actually like to **be** them.
    And your **envy** will be cured.

Gorgeous, **magnificent,** and *sublime* are words that should be
    used as frequently as possible between you and your mirror.
Hubba, hubba is good too. And please never forget to **smile.**

For a long time yet, there will be things
        not to like in time and space . . .
    animal testing, war, discrimination,
        hatred, to name a few.
But please realize, only while living
        can you do anything about them.

When it comes to climbing mountains,
        slaying dragons, or just plain getting what you want,
    remember, you've got a built-in, double-secret advantage:

You're supernatural.

In the truest sense,
        the world around you
            is just more you.

Just because all things are possible,
        doesn't mean you're supposed to do all things.
    Besides, it's not like you aren't going to live forever.

Your **feelings** are your choice,
  what manifests thereafter may not be.
Choose wisely.

Young souls value people for their strength,
  mature souls **value** people for their productivity,
    and old souls value **people.**

Primitive societies live by the Rule of Might,
  and the **strong** prevail.
Advanced societies live by the Rule of Law,
  and the privileged prevail.
Enlightened societies live by the Rule of Love,
  and everyone **thrives.**

Apologize to an old soul
  and your **gesture** will be honored.
Apologize to a young soul
  and matters may become even **more** complicated.
  Apologize **anyway.**

What **if** every wrinkle, scar, and gray hair
    made you more **beautiful?**
Every tear shed, mistake made, and challenge faced
    drew you closer to the light?
And every breath taken, sentence spoken, and path chosen
    sparked uproarious **cheering** from behind
        the curtains of time and **space?**

They do.

Taking **full** responsibility for your life includes
    never forgetting to have **fun.**

The novice **learns** to be honest with others,
    in terms of who, what, when, and where.

The **advanced** soul learns to be honest with self,
and discovers that "perspective" rules, yet changes **swiftly.**

The **master,** however, studies honesty in terms of
motivation, where heretofore, the lies have really piled **up.**

It's **not** what's said that determines whether
    you're being honest, but **why** you said it.
For example, if someone told you it's a beautiful day,
    to distract your attention from the dent they just
put in your car door, they'd be lying.

Never make a **decision** until you have to.

People who give are given to.
    People who care are cared for.
And people who **love** . . .
    age slower, run faster, **jump** higher,
are as happy with friends as they are alone,
    climb more trees, **skip** when they could walk,
kiss when they could talk,
    take the odd Friday off,
experience faster **manifestations,**
    and are really popular with animals.

Being **worthy** isn't something you earn,
    it's something you **recognize.**

Always see work as play
and play as important,
and soon you won't know the difference between them.

A "forever being" would never worry about the future,
look back and regret, or have anything, ever, to fear.
Unless they forgot they're forever.

Upon hearing criticism, the beginner scorns it.
The careful student weighs it.
And the master says, "But, of course!"
understanding she attracted it and therefore
needed to hear it, whether it was true or not.

Never has a word been uttered
that didn't have meaning to the ears who heard it.

Offering criticism belies a longing for
recognition, appreciation, and validation.
None of which, however, can be obtained
through criticism.

Thinking that the death of a loved one is unfortunate,
ill-timed, sad for the departed, or random is to deny
the perfection and order that are otherwise so abundantly
obvious throughout these magical jungles of time and space.

From time to time, as your life allows,
try not to be too practical, logical, or predictable.

Often, that which you misunderstand is drawn to you.
Never because you "needed" the lesson,
nor because all must be so initiated, but because there had
been earlier thoughts of awe, wonder, or criticism.
And such thoughts, as all thoughts must, will rearrange your life
to bring you more of whatever you were thinking of.
And then, in attracting what you didn't understand,
you will ultimately gain enough clarity to understand it,
release it, and finally, be free of it.

Spirituality should not be sought to avoid
the material world, but to better engage it.

Sometimes the **people** who know, don't know they know.
And sometimes the people who don't know, **think** they do.
    But you can always tell who is which,
        because with **knowing** comes kindness.

A test that **reveals** whether or not those in your company
    are truly enlightened is whether or not they **treat**
others as if they, too, are **truly** enlightened.

The **primary** roles of love are not to heal, fix, or mend.
    Not to soothe, cure, or ease.
Not even to refresh, rejuvenate, or restore.
    The primary roles of love are to
        "Yahoo!" "Yee-haa!"
            and "Whoo-hoo!"

The **difference** between a young soul and an old soul
    is only known by the old **soul,**
        who would never breathe a word of it.

The most fun a baby soul can have
  comes from **having.**

The most fun a young soul can have
  comes from **doing.**

And the most fun an old soul can have
  comes from **being**—
    which usually leads to lots of having and doing.

Ultimate life **mastery** eventually becomes
  more a function of knowing **what** to want,
than knowing how to **get** what you want.

It's being **alive** that makes you rich.

If an event was so super-extraordinarily rare
  and **fantastically** incredible
    that it only happened once every 10 *billion* years,
  it would still be infinitely more ordinary, routine,
    and credible than the **passage** of any given day.

An enlightened **soul** is not one
to whom truth has been **revealed,**
but one who has summoned it.

A little heads-up on an affliction
that **afflicts** all really old souls:
Giving love, eventually, becomes a much **greater**
need than receiving it.

Whenever conferring with another—
either face-to-face or across the miles—
whether a human being, departed spirit, or sentient tree,
always speak to the **highest** within them.

(Right, as if some trees weren't sentient. Nice catch.)

When **you** distrust, you **attract** the untrustworthy.

The very first **inkling** you may have
    that you were actually born into "spiritual **royalty**"
comes when you notice there are flowers only you can pick.
    Butterflies only you can **see**.
Laughter and tears only you can know.
    And dreams only you can make **real**.

Let every season run its course and every tide ebb and flow,
    but **think** not that you have no choice
        of where your **wandering** mind may go.

In other words, **letting** life happen
    doesn't mean giving up your **power**.

The **reason** most people worry so much,
    is because there exists between them and **life**
a passionate love **affair**.

If ever **granted** one wish, wish for what is,
    because nothing will ever be **better** than living
in a world where the past doesn't matter,
    the future can be **anything**,
        and your thoughts become **things**.

The **trick** to being in the right place, at the right time,
is knowing you **already** ar**e**.

It always works, there's **only** love,
things are get**ting better,** you chose well,
there've been **no** mistakes, you're never alone,
and everything makes you **more**.

Y**ou** can be quite sure,
given the *infinite* choices available at the time
and your celestial connection with the Divine,
that long ago, when you carefully mapped out your
present adventure into the **jungles** of time and space;
the hills and valleys you would likely traverse;
the setbacks and advances you would likely encounter;
the good, the bad, and the ugly,
and all of the lives you would touch;
when your planning was done
and the "big picture" **revealed** . . .

. . . you **burst** into tears of **joy,**
overwhelmed by its perfection and who you'd become.

Savor the uncertainties.

Seize the possibilities.

Seek.

Wander.

Explore.

Ask.

Face your fears.

Don't rush love

or force details.

Take risks.

Be exceedingly kind.

Move with your dreams.

You have what it takes to

be whoever you feel called to be.

Your full presence is needed;

you were chosen to live amid these very days,

as much as you chose.

You are inclined to succeed

and your success will inspire others to do the same.

You are who God most wanted to be.

the
man
i am

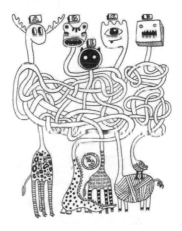

Two years ago, at the local science center, we were both deep into the three-story-tall transparent human-hamster house, that really was for kids taller than you, and not for adults at all. As in earlier visits, your zeal for adventure had us both lost inside. Like usual, hunched over, cramming myself into the barrel hallways and spiral climbs, I was one of the few, if any, parents inside.

Especially endearing were your repeated calls for me to follow you whenever I slowed, your hand blindly reaching behind you to receive mine, "Daddy, Daddy, come on, Daddy!" There was no shame or embarrassment that I was with you. To the contrary, I was the cool enabler of your adventures—besides, you hadn't reached that age yet. Each time you called, the sound of your voice quickened my pace and filled my heart, helping me to forget the physical pain of the assignment.

About an hour into it—an *hour*—my knees and back and neck were so tired, I casually let the space between us increase and you silently "let me slide," aware but ignoring, or so I thought, the distance growing between us.

Before too long, I was on the outside, looking in. When possible, I watched and trailed under you, far above me, though you were no longer reachable. It was clear you were getting quite good at navigating this thing and didn't really need me. Similarly, while the first few times it was fun for me to go inside as the doting, appreciated father, I'd had my fill. From the viewpoint of comfort, yours as much as mine, we probably let our playing and mutual dependency go on longer than necessary. Yet we were both happy to have spent a little extra time together, ensuring attainment of this point between dependence and release. That you'd still call for me from time to time, as if to need me . . . sweet bliss.

Without any warning whatsoever, a trace thought in my mind rapidly grew into a man-eating beast, and suddenly, I was gutted. It happened as you climbed alone up a level, from the second to the third, and began to leverage yourself around an obstacle, not that there was any connection between what you were doing and what I was thinking. It dawned on me that this process leading to independence is exactly what it'll be like once you grow up, ready to leave our home. That the father-daughter relationship is a functional one. A job, fulfilling, joyful—especially joyful—to share life with you, to guide and help you, so that one day you can fly from our home and start your life. Then, too, there'll be some overlap, in between faux dependency and independence, for everyone's comfort. From which your every move will then be about *your own* adventures in the world beyond our home, maybe even with your own kids one day, no longer revolving around your mom and me. That is, if we're even included at all, except for the rare, compulsory family holiday, at which I'll tell those in your life the same old stories and share the same old photos, trying to be relevant, my heart lost in the past, reliving what will surely be the most enchanted memories of my entire life . . . of times you probably won't even remember.

Oh, doth nostalgia work fast! In my mind you were already gone, instead of three years old, inside of a Plexiglas maze. Overcome with a heart-wrenching sadness, two dripping pools of saltwater where eyes once were, with hopelessly blurred vision unable to distinguish between you and other crawling toddlers, a swelling knot in my throat . . . thinking, *WHAT HAVE I DONE?! Lost my mind?! Got a little tired so I let MY BABY scale unreachable heights in the human-hamster house?* Were you really okay? Ready to be on your own? *WHY THE HELL was I in such a hurry to let you drift? Was I in THAT MUCH pain? Couldn't I have been useful just a little longer? Wouldn't it have been worth it to hang around a bit more, prolonging the opportunity TO BE TOGETHER . . . before, IN THE BLINK OF AN EYE, you'd definitely not want your "Daddy" slowing you down?*

On the verge of a loud and embarrassing snort-sob, I spotted you and saw you waver. You stopped mid-tunnel. You spun around, and around again . . . and then, hallelujah, I heard you call, "Daddy . . . ? *Daddy?! Where are you?*"

"HERE I AM!" I waved with an exaggerated, ecstatic grin and eyebrows so optimistically stretched they almost left my face. *Is this really happening?* Or was I having some delusional fantasy? My eyes sharpening their focus, I saw yours lower to find me, truly surprised I had left my post, "*Daddy, WHY DID YOU LEAVE ME?*" You looked as desperate for me as I had been feeling for you. "Daddy, *I NEED YOU!*" My heart burst.

Faster than an Olympian track star, I entered that human-hamster house hunched to half the height of my almost six-foot-three-inch frame, did the loop, ripped a few contortions to ascend the spiral climb, and leapt over the plastic bubble pit to give you a reassuring bear hug before you could say, "DADDY!" one more time. *Sweet* redemption . . .

What *w-a-s* that?

I still don't know, but because of it, I was reminded of how much I love you . . . and love being loved by you. And I suddenly felt again as if all else in my life has existed to reach this moment. Not that any one part, including my love for your mother, is less important, because from all those parts being what they were, this moment was possible. This realization suddenly illuminated all else that came before your birth in an equally glorious, meaningful light. The depth of my love for you is not merely explained and held by *your* existence, but extends to all things, all times, all places, and all the people in my life that brought us here. We are one, they are us, we are them, all is God, God is love—the very embodiment of life's greatest mystery, *answered.*

It seems so obvious now, that the world we live in is one huge human-hamster house that takes us nowhere, except within. The props and technologies we harness are far less important for what they achieve, and far more important because they give us a context in which to create, interact, and be together. It matters not whether we commute every day like the Flintstones or the Jetsons. What's important is that there are people in our lives to learn from, play with, grow with, and love.

That's what we are to each other—mirrors, sounding boards, love switches. It's the drama that makes our lives rich, that fleshes out and gives meaning to our journeys, creating reference points of relativity where none could otherwise exist. *The drama!* Oh my God, how wrong I had it.

Merit, success, money, service, dedication, innovation do not hold a candle to the treasure of emotions that make up our lives.

It's the romance of life, *created by believing in the illusions* that stirs our heart and binds our sense. Our false belief that time, space, and matter are real ultimately shows us that only our feelings last. Just as my false belief that I could lose you ratchets up my appreciation for the present moment, or my false belief that you are "my" daughter fills me with self-love and importance that I might not have otherwise allowed. These false beliefs are like temporary crutches that we will one day walk without. You've shown me this, and more.

Relishing the perfection in you, I began to consider that beyond your digits and health, what I marvel over most is your unique God-illuminated essence, which quite obviously *is present in every little girl . . . and every little boy . . . and, of course, in every grown-up.* That it *must* be there in all people, never wavering, blazing in all its glory. It could be no other way. No matter who, no matter where, no matter when, and just as important, no matter what they've ever done. They still remain of God, by God, *pure God.* That "we are" is our saving grace, the pulsing proof of our divinity. Our magnificence does not exist because of what we do, achieve, or have. That we breathe is enough.

And then . . . when I least suspected it . . . with denial at first . . . then reluctance . . . and finally . . . a shrug . . . *I saw it in me.* I saw that *I am* the very same, pure miracle. Which is what I've written and taught others for years, yet it took my feelings for you, before I really got it about me.

This concept is still expanding in my mind. Especially getting that the love I have for you, which will never wither or fade, must be what *my* parents once felt and *still* feel for me. And more, what God once felt, and *still* must feel, for me. And that like my love for you, their love is not about what I do or don't do, who I am or who I become, not even about who or how much I serve. Their love "is" because *I am* . . . again, the very embodiment of life's greatest puzzle. Leading, therefore, to my ultimate realization:

I already am . . . the man you think I am.

In fact, missing the mark is impossible. I can't not be that person, any more than you could be less than the perfection I'm constantly in awe of. *This is who we really are.* All of us. No one left behind, each a rare and precious spark of God, left to find this out for ourselves, or . . . maybe from our daughter.

Know this for yourself, precious wonder, and remember it should you ever feel unworthy of love. You're already more than you could ever hope to become. You are utterly adored simply for being who you are, exactly as you are, who you can't not be.

Without a doubt, right here and now, as you read these very words with eyes that sparkle, no matter the day, amid your dancing manifestations in a perfect world on an emerald planet while your heart beats, your blood flows, and angels peer over your shoulder, I think that you, and I, and everyone who may ever read these words, and everyone who won't, are the "luckiest" people alive.

I'll love you forever, Solecito, my little sun—

Dad

about the author

Mike Dooley is a *New York Times* best-selling author whose books have been published in 25 languages. He's also a late-blooming first-time husband and father, who's now living and learning between Orlando, Florida, and Manzanillo, Mexico. You can learn more about Mike at www.tut.com.

For a daily dose of brief insights from Mike Dooley, join the 800,000 people who subscribe to his free Notes from the Universe at www.tut.com.

Hay House Titles of Related Interest

YOU CAN HEAL YOUR LIFE, the movie,
starring Louise Hay & Friends
(available as a 1-DVD program, an expanded 2-DVD set,
and an online streaming video)
Learn more at www.hayhouse.com/louise-movie

THE SHIFT, the movie,
starring Dr. Wayne W. Dyer
(available as a 1-DVD program, an expanded 2-DVD set,
and an online streaming video)
Learn more at www.hayhouse.com/the-shift-movie

*THE TOP TEN THINGS DEAD PEOPLE WANT
TO TELL YOU,* by Mike Dooley

All of the above are available at your local bookstore,
or may be ordered by contacting Hay House (see next page).

We hope you enjoyed this Hay House book. If you'd like to receive our online catalog featuring additional information on Hay House books and products, or if you'd like to find out more about the Hay Foundation, please contact:

Hay House, Inc., P.O. Box 5100, Carlsbad, CA 92018-5100
(760) 431-7695 or (800) 654-5126
(760) 431-6948 (fax) or (800) 650-5115 (fax)
www.hayhouse.com® • www.hayfoundation.org

———

Published in Australia by:
Hay House Australia Pty. Ltd., 18/36 Ralph St., Alexandria NSW 2015
Phone: 612-9669-4299 • *Fax:* 612-9669-4144 • www.hayhouse.com.au

Published in the United Kingdom by:
Hay House UK, Ltd., Astley House, 33 Notting Hill Gate, London W11 3JQ
Phone: 44-20-3675-2450 • *Fax:* 44-20-3675-2451 • www.hayhouse.co.uk

Published in India by: Hay House Publishers India,
Muskaan Complex, Plot No. 3, B-2, Vasant Kunj, New Delhi 110 070
Phone: 91-11-4176-1620 • *Fax:* 91-11-4176-1630 • www.hayhouse.co.in

———

Access New Knowledge.
Anytime. Anywhere.

Learn and evolve at your own pace
with the world's leading experts.

www.hayhouseU.com